BILLY'S WAR

By Robert Williams

Foreword

Foreword

The year is 1858. The story is set in Howard County in North Central Missouri. The narrator is William Peyton, an elderly veteran of the War Between the States. From his view at the end of his days, he characterizes the conflict as a most un-civil war in which he was unwillingly involved but who became a hardened killer as he took up the sword of vengeance against those who wronged his family and friends.

"Billy" Peyton begins his story as the 13 year old son and grandson of pioneer homesteaders who have proved up a farm and live there alongside a family of slaves they have gained by inheritance. The families get along well, he says, and do not consider themselves slaves and masters, although they are aware that slaves on larger ranches and "plantations"are sometimes treated far worse than their own, whom they refer to as the "colored Peytons."

But with war comes great tragedies and divided loyalties and tales of revenge and retribution among neighbors, friends and family members. Not all will survive, and those who do are haunted by memories they can never forget. This is only one story among many. but it illustrates in harrowing detail the fiction of glory when greed, injustice and human nature devolve to their basest application. Those who take the pleasures and privileges of a civil society lightly should take heed. It was not always so.

-Marideth Sisco

Author's Note

Before putting pen to paper, as it was written entirely by hand, I spent well over a year researching the subject matter. To the best of my ability and memories, most of the major historical events and locations are reasonably accurate.

I certainly have no qualms about taking liberties with many of the characters, especially my ancestors the Peytons, Walkers and Yates. Family documents and oral histories coupled with my own boyhood memories of life on the Howard County family farm paint a fairly accurate picture of the area and those other lives and times. Many of the characters portrayed are fictional but there are also quite a few of the real heroes and villains whose lives and deeds are recorded in this story.

Special thanks must go to Allison London Smith who provided unwavering support and tolerance for the clutter my research created. Additional thanks to my copy editor Kay Goodnow for her skill and great patience, and true gratitude to my editor Marideth Sisco for her critical eye and powerful mind.

Chapter One

Although I am now older than any man has a
right to be, I remember it as if it were yesterday. The
morning mist had risen revealing what was to be a
beautiful spring day. My morning chores were completed and I figured I could use a rest. My favorite
spot for this activity, or lack thereof, was a large,
freshly cut woodpile of blackjack oak. The sun-
drenched wood emitted a pleasing scent that would
always remind me of this farm. Stretching out on
this makeshift lounge, with my dog Jack by my side,
I surveyed the peaceful landscape. My Ma and Pa,
Durette Henry Peyton and Martha Best, along with
my grandparents, Yelverton and Mildred Peyton, had
moved to Missouri by covered wagon back in 1843
from Kentucky, eventually settling here in Howard
County. They were able to purchase 110 acres right
off and another 110 a few years later. Over the years
the homestead had evolved into a sprawling complex
of buildings, woods and fields I called home.

I continued to bask in the sun even though I was
acutely aware that more tasks awaited me. There
was some activity behind the house in the garden,

but I chose to ignore the labors of the others in my household.

Our house was not as grand as some of our neighbors but I was proud of what my family had achieved. The original log cabin had grown into a two-story clapboard structure. The house was separated from the outbuildings by a large fenced-in yard. Everyone had helped whitewash the house last summer and the board showed snowy white in the bright sunlight.

My Grandpa and Pa had argued for some time over whitewashing the main house. Prior to last summer there was not a speck of paint on any of our buildings which had, to differing degrees, mellowed into a dull gray. Pa maintained that paint was an expensive luxury that vainly advertised one's wealth and he would have nothing to do with this pretense. But when the whole family ganged up on him and Ma said he had better paint it if he knew what was good for him, Pa grudgingly relented.

Off to the right were the barns, a chicken house and corn crib. To the left was our outhouse and beyond that, three small cabins that housed our help.

The kitchen was separated by about eight feet from the main house. This inconvenience was necessary as a fire prevention measure. This was my favorite place since it was warm in winter and smelled of the delicacies that were prepared there. Near the kitchen stood the smoke house and beyond that the root cellar.

The barn was new, raised last year by the family and our near neighbors. It was the heart of the operation. Next to it was the old cow barn, a horse shed and blacksmith shop. Inside the great barn my father had tacked beaver and fox pelts to the wall. These had been hunted and tanned last winter and were intended to become a major source of ready cash when we shipped them down river to New Orleans and beyond. The hog house and lot were furthest away from the house and, of course, away from the prevailing winds.

Out in the fields I could see some folks moving about, clearing the land to plow, I decided. Along with the sounds of the barnyard came the ever increasing laughter of the younger children at play. This finally stirred me from my reveries.

It was time to attend the ever present chores that constantly threatened my leisure. Even though we had our colored 'Peytons,' Pa insisted that we all "carry some of the load." I suppose the Negroes are really Walkers since they came to the family as my Aunt Sophie's dowry. It is of no matter today, but that is how it was then.

In the growing season, the younger children were responsible for tending the pumpkins, gourds, onions, turnips and squash as well as caring for the rows of sweet corn.

Since everyone in the family had assigned jobs, the burden was lifted for each of us which created some free time. My favorite chores were not boring, like carrying water from the well or chopping wood. Instead, along with my older brother Guffey, we cared for the mules and horses. For as long as I could remember I had tended this stubborn pinto pony named Calico. A favorite trick of his was to run near the hedge rows trying to knock me off, but I loved him anyway.

There were not as many of us as some of our neighbors, yet with the addition of our extended family we were becoming a sizable clan.

Besides Ma and Pa, our household consisted of my father's brother's widow Sophie Walker Peyton, her daughters Frances Ann and Ida, and her son, my cousin and best friend Jacob. Jacob and I were about the same age. I was a month older and would turn 14 in June. And then there were my brothers and sisters. Besides Guffey, there was our oldest brother George William and the younger children, Finis Yates, Julia and Millicent.

The matriarch of our Negro family was Aunt Polly who cooked and cared for us. Her daughter Kezzie helped with the household chores. The three older boys were field hands and hired out to other farms and plantations from time to time.

Of them, Rufus was the oldest and smartest, Jebadiah was certainly the strongest and Obadiah (who was about my age) was my second best friend. Jacob, "Obe" and I shared many adventures over the years. Polly's husband Monrow was a skilled blacksmith and folks came from miles around to have him shoe their horses and repair their wagons and farm equipment.

The little family burial ground located down the lane contained the remains of several of Ma's and Aunt Polly's children that over the years had taken sick and died. I didn't remember any of them, but Ma always turned sad when they were mentioned.

The slaves were considered part of the family. Sophie's parents, Jesse and Elizabeth Walker had moved to Randolph County (just north of us) and my Uncle Mitchell had courted and married her. Not long after the last child was born my uncle and her parents took sick and died of cholera. She sold the farm and moved, lock-stock-and-barrel, in with us.

We were happy for the help her Negroes brought, even though healthy slaves could bring over $1,000 each, and she could have sold them. Pa said that Aunt Sophie just couldn't bear to lose any more of her family.

I had recently read an article in a Saint Louis newspaper that said that just a few years earlier,in 1821 , the population of the territory consisted of about 60,000 inhabitants and that 10,000 of these "citizens" were African American slaves.

The editor had speculated that the numbers had grown since then and that the majority continued to live in our Boon's Lick area. Many of my father's associates had large plantations that required a significant labor force.

The United States Congress understood that if Missouri was to enter the Union, it would do so as a slave state. In order to maintain a political balance between free and slave the electorate eventually came up with what became known as the Missouri Compromise where Maine was admitted to the Union as a free state and Missouri as a slave state.

This was interesting historical reading but it didn't much matter to our family. Our way of life continued as usual and I believe it was a good life for all of us. But, you know what they say: "Ignorance is bliss." My Pa, however, would have no truck with ignorance.

Following their marriage in the mid eighteen thirties, George and Martha Yates, bringing with them a superior knowledge of farming and a significant family fortune, moved to Randolph County in Missouri. Land prices had stabilized by this time and George purchased a large tract. The plantation prospered due to his farming abilities along with, as my Pa said, the forty slaves and two white indentured workmen who owed him money. A community developed in the surrounding area which came to be known as Yates, and the master of the household was called by the honorific word Squire, because of his English lineage and lifestyle.

Martha bore him a large family and during the winters, their eldest daughter Millicent, (named after her great grandmother who was buried in Virginia) moved into our household and functioned as our teacher.

There were a few schools located in the larger towns and in St. Louis, but in this remote area, home schooling was the norm (at least for the wealthier and better educated families).

The majority of our neighbors were illiterate and most of the boys in the county,from what I knew, liked it that way. Charley Simpson, a neighbor boy we hunted coons with summed it up when he pontificated about "How he ain't got no need for none of that fancy eddication shit." He maintained that reading and ciphering caused more grief than it's worth. There may be some truth to what poor Charley said, but I am profoundly grateful even today for my father's forethought. My Pa believed that all his children should receive the best education available and fortunately for us, Millicent (or Milly) fit the bill. He also flaunted the 1844 law and insisted that the Negro children attend the sessions along with us.

At 15, Millicent had been given the opportunity to attend an academy for young women (commonly called a finishing school) in St. Louis. She had attended church and activities at Christ Church Episcopal "on the corner of Walnut and Second" she was often heard to say.

Miss Millicent's primary focus was on the Three R's, "Readn', Ritin' and 'Rithmatic." She encouraged us to read from some of the books she borrowed from the Squire, as well as the Holy Bible, the 1662

13

Book of Common Prayer and articles from as many newspapers as she could obtain. The <u>Missouri Gazette</u> and the <u>St. Louis Enquirer</u> were her favorites. The local paper published in Franklin helped fill in the gaps. Politics were of special interest to her, but her involvement in the subject was frowned upon by her peers. "It simply isn't ladylike, and should be left to the men," they would say. Not deterred, she would steep us in the debates of the day. I enjoyed these lively sessions and read everything I could, often into the wee hours of the morning, straining my eyes by the dim light of a coal oil lamp.

I was not especially fond of the mathematical portion of our schooling, but I loved the rest and I loved Millicent. Cousin Jacob was in love with her also and we hated it when she would return to her home at Yates during the spring and summer recess.

Our farm was not far from the historic Boone's Lick Road which wound its way through Columbia, Rocheport and Franklin and on west to the Santa Fe Trail. It was a common event for travelers to stop by at evenings and board with us in our extra rooms. Suppertime was exciting when we had visitors and a ready source of news and gossip.

At the forefront of everyone's conversation was what was going on out west in the Kansas Territory. It seems that eastern Abolitionists centered in Massachusetts had founded an immigrant aid society whose sole purpose was to fill Kansas with like-minded citizens.

On trips to Franklin I had seen these Yankee settlers boarding steamboats and heading up the river. They seemed harmless to me, but Pa and his friends were violently opposed to this migration.

No one at the time could foresee the cataclysmic events that would be created by the old 1820 Missouri Compromise.

Beside making slavery the norm in Missouri, even though only 13% of our citizens were slaves, the compromise banned slavery in the part of the former Louisiana Territory north of the Southern border of Missouri, the 36 30`. Of course our state was the exception. Then the United States Senate passed the Kansas-Nebraska Act of 1854. At this point and as I tell this tale at a time far removed from its happening, a history lesson is in order regarding the infamous compromise and its place in the border troubles, as they came to be known. Here is what we knew at the time.

Instrumental in the creation of the Compromise was our pro-slavery Senator David Rice Atchison. Atchison had been born and raised in Kentucky and had attended Transylvania University in Lexington along with his friend and classmate Jefferson Davis. After practicing law in St. Louis he moved to Liberty, Missouri, just 15 miles from the thriving Westport Landing on the great bend of the Missouri River where the city of Kansas City would one day grow. Among his early accomplishments was the organization of a militia unit named The Liberty Blues and the annexation of the Platte Territory into our own state.

The Kansas-Nebraska Act created two new territories and repealed the Missouri Compromise by allowing the inhabitants to choose for themselves if their territories would be slave or free. Folks called this "popular sovereignty."

Pa said this popular sovereignty was simply the right of the majority of citizens to choose how they wanted to live. He said we had our Negro help and they were doing just fine, and so were the blacks owned by our neighbors. "Why, just look at the Squire," he would say, "He's got nigh on to 60 or so niggers working on his plantation and they are better off than a lot of the poor whites we see hanging out at the Taverns." He continued, getting a little red in the face, "And Mrs. Cynthia Smith, she is the largest owner of slaves in the area, with 106. And right here in Howard County we have Mr. William P. Swinney who has 59 working for him. Those abolitionists are just making trouble for us planters!" In these parts a person who owned over 20 slaves would generally be know as a planter, but only 4% of our neighbors could claim that title. Pa was certainly not one of them, though he saw things their way.

By the early 1850's when I was a boy a fragile peace existed along the Kansas-Missouri border, but this was about to change. Outside influences were at work setting about to disrupt the balance of power between free soil and pro-slavery factions. In order

to establish citizenship in the Kansas Territory, settlers were required to build a residence and live in it.
The Abolitionists in Massachusetts provided the
where-with-all for thousands of New Englanders and
foreign emigrants to flood into the new territory.
Southern planters and speculators conceded that the
Nebraska Territory was a fitting destination for the
new free-state emigrants but believed strongly that,
as was defined in the Missouri Compromise, Kansas
should be open for the use of slave labor.

The New England Company had established several towns in Kansas, the most significant one
named after Amos G. Lawrence, the company's
treasurer. This town, modeled after a New England
village, became the seat of the anti-slavery movement. The Episcopal church and school there were
to become in later years the University of Kansas.
After the passage of the Kansas-Missouri Act Missouri politicians and other slave state supporters became concerned over what they considered to be the
artificial populating of the area by an excessive
number of free state settlers. In order to insure that
pro-slavery emigrants in Kansas were able to protect
their claims against this induced invasion of North-
erners, many "protective" societies were formed. The
Platte County, Missouri Self Defense Association had
as many as a thousand members.

The Northern press named these activists "border
ruffians," but in the early days of the struggles the
leaders were not low-life criminals, but prominent

politicians and leading citizens like David Rice Atchison, Boone's Lick planter Claiborne Jackson and Boone County's Col. Samuel Young. New York Tribune propagandist Horace Greeley, made famous for his "Go West, young man!" quote, is the one who, from his perch thousands of miles away, coined the phrase "border ruffian" when speaking about these established landowners and their activities.

At any rate, tensions increased, free-soilers and pro-slavery advocates began settling their disputes with the gun, and the federal government offered little support. The border became and continued to be a lawless frontier. The first known incident occurred in 1854 when an argument erupted between a pro-slaver and a free-stater. The former apparently insulted the latter, who promptly shot him dead. No legal consequences occurred.

As the conflict escalated, Charles Robinson, territorial Governor at the time, requested help for the Northern emigrants in Kansas from the New England Aid company. The "aid" came in the form of one hundred Sharps Carbine rifles hidden in crates marked "Books." These .54 caliber rifles were state of the art weapons at that time. No other personal sidearm could compare. It soon became clear that the new residents of Kansas were ready for a fight. Several major players emerged during this time period. One of the most significant was James Henry "Jim" Lane. He was a friend of Abraham Lincoln and had served in the Indiana State Legislature prior to moving to Kansas. He soon became embroiled in territorial politics and was elevated to a leadership role.

But the gentleman who was to become the best known personality of the decade was the rabid abolitionist John Brown. In the fall of 1855, Brown and his five sons settled in Osawatomie in the Kansas Territory near the border southwest of Harrisonville, Missouri. A non-legal free state legislature had been formed in opposition to the federally authorized one and Brown was an elected member. He was also a leading member of the local Free State Militia, the Pottawatomie Rifles. Due to some of Brown's questionable activities a Federal Judge issued a warrant for the arrest of Brown and a few of his Pottawatomie companions. Constable James P. Doyle and his two sons were given the task of serving them.

In the meantime rumors of a pro-slavery attack on the town of Lawrence sent the Pottawatomie Rifles to the rescue. This was a short lived adventure because the militia decided to return home. Old Brown had other ideas, however, and led his party on a raid to Doyle's cabin. Brown had his sons execute the senior Doyle with a shot to the head, then the Brown boys hacked Doyle's sons to death with their swords. The raid continued at two other homes resulting in the murders of two more alleged members of the pro-slavery party. All of the massacred victims were prominent and respected well-to-do members of the community. The Browns, who were among the emigrant newcomers, were ragged and poor and could easily have fit into Horace Greeley's description of "border ruffians."

Word of the Pottawatomie massacre ignited the spark of violence as the different factions sought revenge against each other with no end to the conflict in sight. The Brown clan and its followers continued their lawless escapades involving free state activities.

Following a raid on Linn County, Kansas, by over one hundred pro-slavery men lead by the Indian Agent for the Territory, George Washington Clarke, a new "hero" of the free-state movement emerged. James Montgomery, a clergyman and school teacher had migrated from Ohio, via Kentucky and Missouri eventually settling in Kansas in 1854. An abolitionist cut from the same cloth as John Brown, he soon gained a place of prominence in the free-state community. His first major contribution to the cause was by crossing back into Missouri and spying on those who had participated in the raid. Then as a colonel of a militia group, he led a raid into Missouri intimidating and capturing some of Clark's men. He was also responsible for establishing free-state spies among the pro-slavery societies. With the information gained from these sources he was able to keep one step ahead of his enemies. In May of 1858, Colonel Montgomery and his band of vigilantes waged a no-holds-barred war on Missouri slave owners.

Chapter Two

On that fateful day, Cousin Jacob and I had finished lunch and a short nap and were now lazily pecking at the clods in our assigned portion of the garden. We were excited because the family was planning an excursion into Franklin later on in the week to deliver some hemp and check out the steamboat that hauled our hard-earned product down river to the big city of St. Louis. Jacob said he wished he could be a sailor on a steamboat so he could visit all the exotic ports we had read about and studied. I told him that I wasn't all that sure about traveling very far from Boone's Lick.

All of a sudden my dog Jack and the other dogs started barking and running down the lane toward the front gate, by the cemetery. We dropped our hoes and ran out to see what the commotion was all about. In front of a small cloud of dust came a buggy accompanied by two men on horseback. This was exciting, since we could see that our visitors were prominent members of the community.

The buggy drew to a stop in front of us. In it was Squire Yates.

"Afternoon, gentlemen," the driver shouted. "Is your father at home?"

"Yes, sir," I replied. "He's out in the north forty. I'll go and fetch him." Jacob said he would show the men where they could get some water for their horses, and he led the way to the house where my Ma was standing on the front porch. I ran to the barn lot and corralled Calico. Heading off bareback in a spiral of dust and a scatter of rocks, I found my Pa where he was burning stumps. This was something BIG, I was thinking. Really big! I could only remember a few times when Squire Yates had come to call and that must have been for funerals. I prayed nothing had happened to Miss Millicent. I thought I recognized one of the mounted men, but I couldn't remember from where or when.

Our guests began conferring with my father, and talked on until they stayed for supper, served on the great dining room table that had once been used as an operating table when Grandpa Yeverton's leg had been amputated after he was caught in the reins and dragged by a team of terrified mules.)

Ma, Kezzie and the girls served, and the rest of us ate outside and strained to overhear the conversation. We wondered what this visit was all about.

Eventually the men moved to the parlor where some of Mr. Calvin Williams' whiskey was served. Pa said that the Williams family had lived on a hard scrabble track of land about ten miles out of Fayette and could barely make ends meet until they built a still and perfected the art of making whiskey. Apparently the Williams had a knack for turning mash into cash, he'd said, because they were fast becoming wealthy.

In spite of the lateness of the hour, the serious conversation continued on. It was good that the moon was full and the roads would be as light as day. I peeked in the window as Pa passed a jar of his prized home grown Peyton tobacco around for his guests to sample. My older brothers Willliam and Guffey sat quietly in the corner as my Pa puffed slowly on his corncob pipe and listened intently.

To his left, George Yates was seated in the chair of honor, one that had been passed down in the family for generations and had survived the long journey from Kentucky. Next to him was seated the prominent area planter, Claiborne Jackson. The other visitor, I learned later, was in the employ of Mr. Jackson.

I pressed my ear to the open window carefully and eavesdropped on their heated conversation.

"It's plunder, plunder I say. How long can we just sit by and let this happen?" George Yates was speaking. The entire conversation centered on events happening along the western border. The visitors had just learned of the newest action that had brought death, destruction and economic loss to their beloved state. Claiborne Jackson was relaying a conversation he had had with Senator Atchison:

"David Rice said to me, Sir, I have fewer regrets than not ending the life of that damned John Brown when I had the chance." The chance had been at the battle of Osawatomie when Atchison's militia forces had chased Brown's men from the area.

Yates added, "Yes, too bad that was. But what about that damned preacher Montgomery? He and his band of nigger-stealing cutthroats are the problem. Here and now! If that sonofabitch ain't stopped it will be the end of life as we know it."

Then my Pa said, "I hear there is an organization set up by those Free-staters called the 'Underground Railroad.' It's said they steal negroes from their homes and carry them up north to Iowa. Imagine that, taking poor folks from their families and homes."

Claiborne Jackson spoke as he refilled his cup with Pa's Boone's Lick whiskey: "You must have heard about that other damned preacher up in St. Louis a few years back. No? Well, his name was Eli Lovejoy. I don't know what denomination he was part of, but he certainly was not an Episcopalian!"

The listeners grunted their approval. Jackson continued, "He was one of those God almighty righteous abolitionists, stealing slaves and not minding his own business. He set up this printing press and spewed his bile all over town. Well, the law-abiding citizens of that great city ran him out of town. So he set up shop across the river in Illinois. Some Missouri folks slipped over there to toss that damned press into the mighty Mississippi but he started shooting at them. In the end the poor reverend was sent straight to hell with five bullets in his holier-than-thou self."

Claiborne Jackson added, "This damn Montgomery isn't satisfied with stealing our help. His outlaws will also take horses, wagons and everything they can carry off. My property, your property, our capital, is slave property. These bastards are attacking our financial holdings and the solvency of our businesses. If they are allowed to get away with those raids south of the river in Bates and Cass counties it won't be long before they are burning the barns and slaughtering the stock here in Howard County." And, he said, "the conflict could easily spread on northward and endanger Gov. Price's holdings. Then there'd be hell to pay."

He reminded them that former Governor of Missouri Sterling Price, who had served from 1853 until 1857, had a plantation north of Howard County in Chariton County which was considered one of the largest in the area.. Price owned many slaves and had consistently fought against the abolitionist movement. As events along the southwestern border of the state were heating up, the long standing so-called "civil war" was spreading, and as it spread, becoming even less civil. Though the free-staters in Kansas were true believers in the abolitionist movement there was also ample evidence to suspect that some of the reasons behind their raids on Missouri farmsteads were not motivated by the lofty and noble goal of freeing Missouri slaves. All too often the destitute Kansans were drawn to the wealth of their Missouri neighbors, and using the slavery issue to simply rob and steal.

Most of the flames of violence and plunder, Jackson contended, were being fanned by a resident of Mound City, Kansas. Charles Rainsford "Doc" Jennison equaled his colleague James Montgomery in aggressive violence by killing farmers, stealing their corn and livestock, burning their buildings and stealing their slaves for emancipation to Canada through the underground railroad. No one and no thing was safe from the raiders in Vernon, Bates, Cass and Jackson Counties.

Having made their case for impending disaster if no action was undertaken, the plan that Squire Yates and the others presented to my father, Durette Peyton, was a simple one. These planters, along with Senator Atcheson and former Governor Price would solicit assistance in raising volunteers to augment the militia so they could "once-and-for-all" put a stop to what the eastern press was calling the "Border War."

My Pa told them he would do what he could to recruit men from the local area, but the responsibilities of caring for his farm precluded his personal involvement and that of his older sons.

What he said next took the wind out of my sails for a spell. He said that even though we were too young to fight, he would send me and my cousin Jacob on the expedition. We could tend the livestock, do chores and run errands. "It would be a good experience for them and perhaps they would learn something," he said. I was less than thrilled, but Jacob was beside himself. Now he could finally get to ride on a steamboat. The expedition was to form up at Franklin, move west to Platte County by riverboat and train with militia there, with the intent of eventually heading south for a confrontation with the free state forces. There had been many hostile acts over the years, but it was hoped that this would be the attack that would put an end to the hostilities. It seemed especially important at this time because of the escalation of violence and the failure of the federal government to provide troops to police the area. Even though we were expected to be noncombatants, we packed our weapons along with the other materials we supposed we would need for a trip of a couple of months. Like all farm boys, we had hunted since a very early age and were considered to be above average shots. Jacob would pack his deceased father's shotgun, a .20 gauge double barrel percussion instrument. I would rely on my old but cherished 1802 Harpers Ferry .54 caliber flintlock rifle.

* * *

The day of departure was sunny and relatively mild. It had rained the night before and the land was a vibrant green. The plan was for Pa to load the whole family in the farm wagon and haul us to the landing at Franklin Town. The Negroes said their goodbyes. Aunt Polly and Kezzie were in tears and Obe said he wished he could come with us. Off we went, down the lane, past the cemetery, out into the main road toward our great adventure. The trip to the landing was a festive affair, even though Ma and Aunt Sophie looked as if they might be having second thoughts about the wisdom of this adventure. The rest of the family seemed to be happy for us, and Guffey presented me with a powder horn that he had made especially for me. I think Jacob was a bit jealous, but the prospect of a steamboat trip quickly overshadowed any negative feelings he might have had.

The steamboat ride up river was as exciting as Jacob had imagined, especially when we got stuck on shifting sandbars or hit by drifting brush and logs. We had lived near the river all our lives but it was exciting to travel part of the historic journeys that the expedition of Lewis and Clark and the Corps of Discovery had followed.

The boat ride also exposed us to many debates on a wide selection of topics. I was fascinated by the discussions but Jacob would rather explore the boat. Religion and new technology were trumped, however, by a variety of political opinions. Not everyone supported the institution of slavery, but to a man this gathering hated the Kansans and their attempts to force their abolitionist views on Missourians.

Through our teacher Millie, we had been good students of the events that brought us to this stage in our lives. But little did we know that Senator Stephen Douglas' Kansas-Nebraska Act would completely change our lives or perhaps even end them.

There was a great deal of talk among the new recruits regarding the last big raid in 1856, two years prior. I heard how Claiborne Jackson, the very man who had sat in our family parlor and who was directly responsible for our current adventure, had put his campaign for Congress on hold long enough to lead over a thousand armed Missourians to Lawrence, Kansas, to vote in the territorial election to keep Kansas a slave state.

I listened intently to hear how in the spring of that year another band of pro-slavery men launched yet another attack on the city of Lawrence, ransacking the state buildings and newspaper offices and burning the hotel which was the headquarters for the Free State Supporters. A great deal of looting took place but no one was killed, or so it was said.

It was the current consensus of those on the riverboat headed upstream to Lexington that this "lawlessness" was justified since it came nowhere near to the damage, murder and theft that had been perpetrated by the free state Kansans.

I told Jacob, after hearing one of these long hate filled discussions, "I just don't know about this. We get all upset about the injustices of the Kansas raiders and they come back with the same comments about us. 'Bushwhackers.' That's what they call us, Jacob, bushwhackers!"

Jacob said "Well, Billy, I guess that's what we are. I don't see nothing wrong with being a bushwhacker if it's the right thing to do. They is the ones who is breaking the law. The Federal law and for Pete's sake, God's law. It just ain't right, and I for one am proud to be a bushwhacker!"

I said, "I guess I am a bushwhacker whether I want to be or not. Look at us. We're just about to get into the biggest mess of our lives. Kind of exciting, ain't it? Bushwhackers! Who would have ever thought it?"

Chapter Three

Stepping aside for a moment from my personal memories as occasionally I must, I will remind you again of where we were in History. In February of 1857, President James Buchanan had recommended that Kansas be admitted to the Union as a slave state and the senate approved this on the condition that it would be supported by popular vote.

This situation energized men like James Montgomery and other free-stater emigrants to increase their efforts at ridding Kansas of those pesky unwanted pro-slavery voters, most of whom were already established residents before the emigrants arrived. We knew this in theory, but we would soon see it on the ground. In the meantime, we boys were being offered a much wider view of our home country than we had ever before experienced

As we continued upriver I was amazed at the abundance of crops that spread out before us in the fertile river bottom. Corn was almost a foot high and there was an variety of other crops – hemp, wheat and tobacco – sprouting up. It looked as if hundreds of Negroes were tending the fields.

Many fine homes rimmed the bluffs above the river and it seemed that prosperity reigned in this section of our state.

At our stop in Glasgow the news arrived that the residents of Harrisonville had requested that our current Governor, Mr. Robert Stewart, provide the citizens with arms so they could defend themselves. We heard that several militia companies were forming in Cass and Bates Counties and our force forming at Liberty was preparing to add assistance to the beleaguered citizenry. We eventually arrived at the landing In Liberty and found our way to the newly formed militia bivouac. I grew more excited by the hour since we were now part of a real live expedition. We would make history and bring about peace. That's what we told ourselves.

More and more men filtered into camp and the leaders struggled to bring about some form of military order. Men were assigned to different companies and we started to settle into the routine. We chose to affiliate with a company comprised of Randolph and Howard County volunteers who welcomed us and made us feel at home. Our primary duties were caring for the companies' mules and looking after a small herd of cattle that had been donated to feed our troops. Generally those who owned their own horses preferred to look after them themselves, so our task was not as great as it might have been.

We soon discovered that the camp could get a bit rowdy by the fires in the evenings. Whiskey would be passed around and some tall tales spun. I had tasted whiskey but didn't much care for it. Pa's was certainly smoother than the rough liquid our companions shared, but Jacob consumed it with gusto. I knew he would be sorry come tomorrow.

We were barely fourteen, and most of our campfire companions were just a few years older. We enjoyed this exposure to a world much bigger than Howard County. We were also improving our cussing abilities.

One night, following a swig or two of John Barleycorn, Nate Pierson, who hailed from over by Boonville and who was a veteran of the big raid on Lawrence, relayed his experience to the wide eyed young listeners.

"Yep," said Nate, "It was some doing. Them free-soilers in Lawrence had them a fright. There was dang near a thousand of us Missouri folk over there, You boys said your Pa was a friend of Claib Jackson, well, he was in charge of the lot of us.

"Oh, and did you know that Claiborne has married three sisters in succession? Yep, their daddy was Dr. John Sappington who made it rich selling them quinine pills for malaria. The story goes that when Claiborne came for the third daughter, Sappington said 'I reckon you'll be back next time for the old woman!' Ain't that something? "Anyway, Jackson gathers us all together and gives this big speech telling about how the voting law in the Kansas Territory is vague and said that we had just as much right to vote there as them outsiders. So we did, and then we hightailed it for home."

Jacob said, "Well how did it turn out?"

Levi Summers, a young man from Franklin piped in: "Well, it couldn't have been much of an outcome cause we is still fighting for the cause."

Nate said, "Yep! We all figured it was good, but the Free-soilers complained that everything was fraudulent and the territorial governor was scared to death because he was caught in the middle. And you're right, there we were and here we are"

Another man, short, well-dressed and articulate, added, "I know the rest of the story, if you care to hear it." Everyone said that they did. "It unfolded this way," he said. "The territorial governor of Kansas at that time was a man by the name of Reeder who had been appointed by President Pierce. We maintained to him that our voting was no more outlandish than the Kansans. Furthermore, we threatened to hang him if he caved in to their demands. Not long after the voting, our man from here in Platte County, Senator Atchison, called on President Pierce and gave his side of the story. Keep in mind that Pierce is honest but somewhat easy to persuade. He believed the senator's reporting, but didn't want to act without hearing Reeder's side. He is feeling tremendous political pressure from both sides, you understand. Then Reeder arrived in Washington City and told the President what happened.

To Reeder's dismay the President said that all he hears are complaints from the territory and that he blames the Emigrant Aid Society and that furthermore, the Abolitionists are destroying the Democratic Party and that all this bickering could bring on a real civil war. Pierce believed that both sides of the conflict had stuffed the ballot boxes." I asked, "What happened then?"

"Nothing," the knowledgeable stranger replied, "You know how it is with politicians, they just ignore things and hope that they will go away."

"Mister," I said, "There's just so much of this just doesn't make sense to me. How come it is if one of those free-state folks gets killed all hell breaks loose, but if one of us gets murdered they say it's our just desserts?"

Jo Shelby, one of the wealthier men in the county rose from the stump he had been sitting on, brushed off his pants legs and said, "Young man, when you discover the answer to that question, you let me know. Thanks for the whiskey, gentlemen, but I fear I must return home to Waverly. Good evening."

It would be several years before I would see this short in stature but tall in intellect man again.

*　　*　　*

Our journey down south seemed like an eternity. We had never walked so far in our lives. We hopped rides on wagons when we could, but at the end of each day we fell exhausted on our bed rolls and dreamed of the comforts of home we had left so far behind.

One night I was feeling a little homesick so I decided to write a letter to my folks. As I recall, it went something like this:

Dear Ma and Pa, and everyone,

Just a note to let you know we are fine. There is a postmaster in Harrisonville where I will send this, but we will probably be home before it reaches you.

When we passed through Westport the dust was so thick we could hardly breathe. We passed the Old Santa Fe Trail, but continued south instead of going into the Kansas Territory. There are about a hundred of us in our company and we have been told that our job is to help keep the peace in these parts. The land is rich, rolling prairie but sparsely settled. We've seen some burned out homes that housed some prosperous folks before the Kansans got to them.

We have also passed several camps of people who were chased out of Kansas by the Free-staters. They were so happy to see us and begged us to help them regain their land.

It rained a little last night, but we slept under a wagon and kept dry. I hope everyone is fine and Jacob sends his love. Tell Aunt Polly I really, really miss her cooking. And Ma's, too!

Love, Billy.

The company settled in just outside of the village of West Point on the border between Bates County,

Missouri and Linn County, Kansas, just north of the
Marais des Cygnes River, and there we heard this
story.

Earlier that year, Colonel James Montgomery,
who had relieved so many pro-slavery farmers in
Kansas and Missouri of their possessions, with a
large band of vandals, rode into West Point creating
fear in the residents and stealing whatever they
wanted. On their way through the county they
stopped at the home of a farmer named Jack Clark,
robbing him of his valuables and cash. Some of the
men even stole his wife's clothing. The same raid relieved the Rev. George Geyer of his horses as well as
plundering numerous other citizens along the way.

Upon arriving in Bates County, our company
teamed up with a guard unit named the Pleasant Hill
Rangers after the town of the same name. A large
portion of the border area was depopulated due to
the marauding of Montgomery and his men. There
was fear that even with the reinforcements there
would not be enough men to stave off further at-
tacks.

Jacob and I, along with some other Howard
County men, joined up with a pro-slavery force under the leadership of Charles A. Hamilton. It was an
extremely warm day as we set out towards Rich Hill,
Missouri. We were thrilled to be part of the Hamilton
party raiders. We were now not just the boys who
tended the livestock, we were militia men setting out
to right the wrongs perpetrated by that criminal

Montgomery. We had been loaned horses which elevated our mood more than ever.

On our way we met up with a number of folks who had been driven from their homes. It was an angry meeting and everyone's tempers flared. Thirty two of us mounted our horses and rode the short distance to the Kansas community of Trading Post where earlier Montgomery had ransacked the store and dumped barrels of whiskey that were stored there. Mr. Hamilton had compiled a list of men he intended to arrest for their notorious crimes. Among the wanted men there was a blacksmith by the name of Charles Snyder. Hamilton confronted him but the smith would have no part of what he considered to be a ridiculous warrant. He refused to submit to arrest.

One of our party named Bell handed me the reins of his horse and headed towards Snyder. Out of the blue Snyder pulled a gun and before our very eyes shot Bell. I had never seen anything like this before. One minute Bell was laughing and talking about the waste of all that whiskey and the next he was laying there in the dust with a puzzled look on his face. And then he just up and died. Dead! I damn near wet myself I was so scared. That was my first experience of men killing men, but it certainly was not my last. I'm sorry to say it now, but over the years I kind of got used to it.

Hamilton flew into a rage and ordered his posse to march our free state prisoners down to a dry ravine. Our boys lined them up on the bank and shot them all.

I couldn't believe what was happening. I was still in shock over the death of Bell. That was terrible in it's own right, but at least Snyder was fighting in self defense. And now this. Shooting unarmed men in cold blood. It was more than I could comprehend. Four men were killed immediately and six were wounded. I later learned that a seventh man saved his life by pretending to be dead. The blacksmith escaped and was never found. Following the massacre, we received word that Governor Stewart had become concerned enough to dispatch General Parsons of the Missouri Militia to the area. In Harrisonville he established a unit called the Cass County Guards. He then moved on south, creating four more companies of militia.

Most of the hardened militia members were unmoved, believing that justice had been served. After all, these Kansanss had been responsible for dragging these folks from their homes and taking everything they owned, including their dignity.

On the way back to our militia camp I leaned over and threw up. "I just can't do this no more," I said.

"Let's go home," Jacob whispered.

Chapter Four

Our decision was final. We had made up our minds to leave. I was fairly certain that Pa would understand our motivation behind leaving the expedition. We knew we weren't cowards, but we weren't murderers either, even if the cause was a noble one. We had no money so passage on a Westport steamboat was out of the question. We didn't want to tell our plans to our companions in fear of being branded deserters, so we just slipped away in the dark.

Loaded with as much bacon and biscuits as we could safely steal we followed the country roads and trails that we hoped would eventually take us back to Howard County. Walking was no problem since it seemed as if we had walked enough to go to the moon and back already.

The weather was absolutely perfect for our continuing adventure. We believed we could rely on the customary hospitality practiced by the settlers out here on the frontier to help feed and shelter us. Just like back home, travelers could always expect a warm welcome from the families who lived along the way. The only problem was that in this area settlers were few and far between.

As we trudged northeast the terrain changed from the rolling prairie into wooded hills and fertile valleys. On the map we copied back at the Militia headquarters wagon I had estimated that "as the crow flies" we had a little under one hundred fifty miles to cover. Unfortunately, it didn't take long for us to discover we weren't crows.

Up and down, up and down, over creeks and along rivers, sometimes swimming but usually wading across fords that had been located and marked by earlier travelers. It was readily apparent to us that the settlers here were not as prosperous as those in the slave holding counties. In fact, these hill people seemed to be a whole different breed. They lived in small simple cabins and farmed the river valleys.

You see our people back north of the river were emigrants from the mid south, English, mostly, who had sold land and cattle in order to move here, and lived in relative luxury. These people had emigrated more recently from Scotland and Ireland with little more than the clothes on their backs and were just finding their way toward economic security. They were truly a different breed from us. Different ways, different customs, different ideas. Again, that's part of the history.

But whatever their ilk, at every farm and settlement we found that we were welcomed with open arms. We earned our keep by helping out with the chores, chopping wood and toting water. What puzzled me was how these people reacted to our story. They just could not believe that we had been sent on an expedition to help out some people who were so far away from our own home.

One old grizzled farmer who shared his meager meal of fatback and beans remarked, "It's about all we can do to take care of ourselves. We ain't got no time or inclination to go running off to help them rich folks."

I'm sure that this was true in his case since he and the haggard woman he called his wife had ten children. Some were older than we were, but most were younger. One of the girls pointed out a mound surrounded by cedar trees and said that they had buried several brothers and sisters there. They were a ragged bunch and not very handsome to look at, but Jacob seemed to hit it off with one of the girls.

We soon found ourselves deep in the woods along an ancient river. Back in pre-settlement times, this area had been home to the fierce Osage tribe and their allies, the Missouri tribe. We were told that disease and the white man's superior firepower had driven them away.

There were times when we encountered no farms or settlements at all in an area, but in a way, this was more appealing. It felt good to be self sustaining. We had some corn meal and shooting a rabbit or squirrel was no problem since we were skilled young marksmen. The weather held, hot and dry, so our travel was not interrupted by storms. On the tenth day we reached the Village of Osceola, named for the famous Indian chief.

I found work there helping a blacksmith and Jacob cut wood for a widow woman who let us stay in her spare room and sleep on a bed with a straw mattress. We had not experienced such luxury in months.

After a few days we were able to hook up with a party of teamsters who were hauling grain up north. This meant that we could ride part of the way. We left our new found friends eventually at a town in central Missouri called Otterville and struck off again on our own. This was a wealthy area of large farms, and substantial herds of cattle and livestock. Many of the people spoke little English and resembled the German communities we were familiar with farther north, near the Missouri River. In a strange way, this was comforting to us, easing our growing homesickness. It would not be long now before we would be smelling the sweet aroma of buttermilk biscuits. We had been on the road for about three weeks and longed for home.

At Boonville we encountered some neighbors from Howard County, over across the wide, wild river, who paid our toll and rode with us to Franklin. By now we were a sight! Our clothing was threadbare but we were in extraordinary good health. The adventure had removed any echo of baby fat. We were tanned and strong, and much wiser to the ways of the world than we were just months ago when we left from this very landing.

It was summer now, the hay was being cut and raked along with all the other activities required to prepare for winter. The caterpillars had been extra fuzzy this year and the old timers forecasted that the winter of '58 would be a hard one.

*   *   *

On our arrival home, Jacob and I were welcomed back with open arms and Pa said he was glad to have us home safe and sound. I worried that folks would think less of us for leaving the militia but Pa said we had done our part and we were not to worry about it. And that's just what we did as we settled back into the daily routine of life on our farm.

Obe, my next best friend, and I were working the hay field, raking the straw into a giant mound. He stopped, and mopping sweat and hay dust from his face he asks, "Massa Billy, I guess you had rather be off chasing them Kansas folks than stuck here wif me?"

"Naw," I replied, "That wasn't all that much fun. You've heard us go on and on about what we done and what we've seen. But you ain't never said what you thought about it. Before we left you said you would like to go with us. I'm sure glad you didn't, 'cause you might have been killed. I'm not kidding."

Obe says, "Billy, I don't much think it's my place. It don't got much to do wif me. I jes don't understand why all the commotion about running off to Iowa or some place. I think them niggers is crazy. I mean, here on the farms we got work and roofs over our heads and plenty of food and our family, I jes don't understand it. Now, Jebediah, he's such a hot head, always talking about starting a new life. Shit!"

I leaned on my pitchfork. "Obe," I said, "I found out a lot of things on that trip. I found out that most of what we hear from them politicians, and most of what we read in the papers is just plain bullshit. Those free-state folks have been wrong and done some terrible things, but so have we. It's just like Miss Millicent says, 'two wrongs don't make a right.' And I just don't know. You and your folks are family to me. But somehow, it don't seem right for folks to own folks. I guess that if Aunt Sophie was approached and asked to let you all go north she would do that. It would be a big burden for us here at the farm, but I believe Pa and Aunt Sophie would give you your freedom if that's what your folks would want. Or maybe, let you all buy your freedom. Then you could stay here and be share croppers if you didn't want to leave."

Obe took a swig of water from the earthenware jug we carried with us. He plopped down in the shade of the growing hay mound and earnestly said, "Massa Billy, you best be careful what you say. You know how things is. We is happy here. We don't want no changes. Just ask my Ma and Pa, ask Rufus and the girls. This is a good life for us. Now listen, Billy, and this is the truth. We hear talk about what goes on in some of those big plantations. Sometimes I can understand why a negro would want to run away north. The worst part is being sold away from your family, or being sold to them people in Mexico. I feel for them and I know it ain't right. I hear about slaves who want to be free to choose how to live. I hope that will happen. But that ain't us. We happy. We good. You best be keeping your ramblings to yourself." He then picked up a handful of straw and threw it at me and the chase was on.

Time marched on and the memories of our expedition faded somewhat. It was now 1858 but the hostilities along the border still festered. The perpetual rabble rouser John Brown was stirring up trouble again.

According to the news, Brown and his clan activated the underground railroad by riding into Vernon County, Missouri, and "freeing" eleven slaves and liberating the owners of wagons and livestock as well.

One man in Vernon County was killed as he sought to protect his property, including his slaves. And here's some more history to put things in perspective, at least from our point of view:

The stealing of a person's legally held property was not received cordially and created a great deal of fear and anxiety in that Missouri county farther south along the border. Just the mention of old

John Brown could raise the hairs on the back of the neck of the bravest pro-slavery settler.

Throughout the year of 1859 conditions continued to worsen along the border. The hostilities were far from over for these residents. To the relief of most Missourians, John Brown had moved his abolitionist activities out east. For five years Brown, with the ferocity, of an old testament prophet, had followed his abolitionist path of violence in Kansas and Missouri. Then he took the battle eastward.

In October of 1859, far from the ravaged Missouri border, John Brown and his followers attempted to capture the federal arsenal at Harpers Ferry, Virginia. The venture failed and he was captured by federal marines under the command of Colonel Robert E. Lee and Lt. J. E. B. Stewart. When hanged for treason the abolitionists in the north considered Brown a hero and martyr for the cause. The Missourians who had suffered under his crude and ruthless treatment rejoiced at his demise.

*   *   *

By now it was 1860 at the Peyton Farm. We had settled down for the long, wet, cold winter. It was the start of a new decade, one that would eventually change everyone's life. But for now on the farm, life seemed normal. School was back in session and Miss Yates was back holding forth in the Peyton parlor. The three R's had continued to be the focus of our education during the day, although the evenings were filled with lively debates over current events. The colored folks had gone to their cabins so a free and far-ranging discussion over the slavery issue often dominated the conversations. Of course politics was on the minds of everyone in the area since 1860 was an election year.

General unrest on the border and the threat of further aggressive acts upon the citizens of Platte County by the Kansas militias had prompted the continued development of Missouri militia units throughout our homeland and beyond. Our family joined a loosely knit militia that drilled when the weather permitted at Fayette, the county seat of Howard County. After Pa, Guffey and George joined up, Jacob and I argued with my Pa about being allowed to enlist also.

At first he forbade us to get involved. He said he was keenly aware of what we had been through and the terrible execution of those unarmed men we had witnessed back in the spring of '58. It seems he was also aware that the possibility of Jayhawk raids in the county might be a reality. The term "Jayhawking," which was said to have been coined by the Irish emigrant Pat Devlin after a raid into Missouri, came to be a common reference to these Kansas renegades. It seems Devlin returned to Linn County, Kansas with saddle bags filled with ill-gotten "spoils of war." When asked how he had obtained these treasures he said that he had "jayhawked" them. He explained that back in the old sod there was a bird that worried its prey before killing it. That devilish Irish bird was a Jayhawk.

We eventually persuaded Pa that the discipline and training we would receive in the militia would be beneficial and far outweigh the negatives.

Colonel Townsend was our militia leader. He had participated as a young lieutenant in the war with Mexico and had taught our fledgling soldiers a great deal. The precision drill and discipline coupled with his knowledge of the appropriate conduct of combatants far exceeded our experience with the undisciplined rabble we had marched with in Bates County.

Very few of the militia members had regulation arms. The colonel and several of the officers owned sabers and the new 1855 .588 caliber Springfield Rifles. Colonel Townsend also owned the most beautiful brace of 1851-issue, .36 caliber Navy pistols I had ever seen. Others carried a variety of firearms. The farm boys from less prosperous places still carried flintlocks. Most drilled with their shotguns or squirrel rifles. All in all, it was a positive experience for us and for a time the winds of war remained far to the west of Howard County.

On the positive side of the register the commotion stirred up by that rabble rouser John Brown and company had simmered down a bit. Due to a financial depression experienced by the Kansas settlers, many decided to pull up stakes and go back east. Other more adventurous souls decided to join the

Williams

thousands who were traveling west to Colorado and beyond. The huge overland freight company, Russell, Majors & Waddell had started what folks called the pony express. A letter from St. Joseph to Sacramento, California, could be received in just an amazing ten days. Jacob and I talked about maybe signing on as jockeys. We would only have to ride twenty-five mile intervals.

The pro-slavery Mayor of St. Joseph, M. Jeff Thompson, sent the first rider westward on April 3, 1860. We would be sixteen years old in June and certainly old enough, but Pa said we were needed here, and I guess he was right.

But let's don't forget about Mayor Thompson, because he would play a major part in the political and military events that would eventually engulf the state of Missouri. Thompson was a transplanted Virginian steeped in the culture and traditions of the old south.

On the downhill side a drought burned crops and dampened the prospects of increased prosperity for hard working planters. And, of course, there were the upcoming elections, which consumed the thoughts and actions of the planters and landed gentry. Distant but powerful forces were starting to influence events closer to home. "All politics are local" is a common cliché, but it was proving to be true in the lands along the Mississippi and Missouri rivers.

Over on the Kansas-Missouri border, the old enemy to Missouri slave holders, James Montgomery, was rattling his saber again. In order to combat this perceived threat Missouri's Governor Stewart began arming local militias. The unit based at Fayette received several crates of Springfield Rifles because of this, but we still drilled with our own weapons. The governor was accurate in his fears. James Montgomery had been reported to have linked up with a dangerous abolitionist city slicker by the name of Charles "Doc" Jennison, now a colonel in a Jayhawk unit. These two organizers of Kansas vigilante groups were not only a concern for Missourians because of their military might, but for their involvement in the fledgling Republican party as well.

The National Party was formed from abolitionist northern Democrats and members of the old Whig Party who supported free labor. These Whigs divined the future and saw industrialization rather than a plantation economy. That meant trouble for us, and possibly disaster for the larger planters.

Chapter Five

Again we must pause for a history lesson. Here is another scenario of the times and how things got that way.

The Democrat James Buchanan had assumed the presidency in 1856. His predecessor, Franklin Pierce, had waffled over the slavery issue and Buchanan had followed in his wake. The Republican candidate for president in 1860 was an Illinois attorney and former Whig Abraham Lincoln.

The German community wanted their local favorite, prominent St. Louis lawyer Edward Bates as the candidate. Lincoln won the nomination, but creatively soothed their political consciousness by saying that if elected he would appoint Bates as Attorney General and local lawyer Montgomery Blair as Postmaster General.

Montgomery's brother was the powerful politician U. S. Congressman Frank Blair, Jr. The Blair brothers father, Frank Blair Sr., was a friend of Andrew Jackson and one of the founding fathers of the Republican Party in Missouri. Frank Blair, Sr. was related to the famous Missourian Thomas Hart Benton,

founder of the <u>St. Louis Enquirer</u> back in 1818.
Benton was also known for a political difference with
Charles Lucas which ended in a dual on Blood Island
in the middle of the Mississippi River. As a crowd
watched from an ancient Indian burial mound in St.
Louis, Benton shot Lucas dead.

Frank Blair, Jr. had experienced a rather sporadic
education, having been expelled from Yale, North
Carolina and Princeton. Though a bit of a brawler,
having shot someone at Princeton, his political career thrived. He was related to Joseph Shelby, the
same man who had shared our campfire back at Lexington, though they had radically different politics.
Shelby had a large plantation at Waverly that functioned with slave labor. Blair was a city slicker who
rode on his popular father's coattails. Blair, however,
was not cut from the traditional abolitionist's cloth.
His objection to slavery was an economic one. His
idea was to send the blacks to colonies in South
America in order to enable whites to enter the work
force in their place. Humanitarian concerns for the
betterment of enslaved people did not seem to be his
concern. Outside of his circle of friends in St. Louis,
Blair was not a popular figure. Republicans were not
either at that time in Missouri.

By 1860 a dramatic increase of new immigrants
from the northern United States and European
countries had occurred. Rural Missourians still held
to their ancient southern ways, but the newcomers

were bringing new political ideologies along with their old languages.

In appearance, Frank Blair resembled a southern planter by sporting a drooping mustache and handsome goatee, but that is where the resemblance ended. Blair had made powerful allies in the German community and he used this to great advantage. He organized his German followers into a paramilitary group called the "Wide Awakes." This militia group prepared to fend off aggression from the pro-slavery factions as well as act as his own personal bodyguard.

Meanwhile in our neighborhood, at a political rally held in the Boone's Lick residence of Claiborne Jackson, my father Durette Henry Peyton entered the debate. There were several powerful planters present who proclaimed Vice President Breckenridge to be the next messiah, but my Pa protested: "My friends, I am aware of the possibilities of economic stress upon all of us. Yes, I concede many of you will suffer more than me, however, consider this. I have heard you vilify Mr. Lincoln tonight, and to most of what has been said, I agree. But I ask you to consider this. If Mr. Breckenridge is elected war will surely come. Gentlemen, we are not ready for war. My sons and neighbors drill in our militia unit on a regular basis, but we lack modern weapons. We lack factories and resources, we even lack in numbers when compared to the resources of the Yankees."

There was a murmuring in the room. Several stood to object. Pa raised his calloused hand and in an authoritative voice seldom heard when he spoke, he continued: "Gentlemen, please hear me out. You have spoken. Now it's my turn. So, now consider this. If Mr. Lincoln is elected what will happen? He says he will leave the slave states alone, that even though he is against the institution his primary, no his main interest, is in protecting the union. But we all know what will happen. Those damnable abolitionists will take over. They can't be contained. And it will be our border war all over again on a wide scale. We are again faced with the prospect of war against an unbeatable enemy. What are we to do? It's the proverbial position between a rock and a hard place. For me and mine, the place of least discomfort is the platform presented by Mr. John Bell. Bell is well known. He has fought this battle for many years. He is my candidate. Thank you, gentlemen, I rest my case."

By now Claiborne Jackson had thrown his planters hat into the political ring, running for Governor. But politics are seldom cut and dried. Differing factions must be dealt with, coalitions formed. Jackson found himself caught in the middle. He was a wealthy slaveholder with thousands of acres under cultivation on his plantation so, it goes without saying where his allegiance lay. In so many ways he was a Breckenridge man, a secessionist, a supporter of the pro-slavery platform. But he was also a shrewd businessman and politician. The tea leaves he read led him into an alliance with the Douglas Democrats.

But at the Missouri Democratic Convention in April of 1860, Breckenridge prevailed and a strong proslavery platform was adopted. The convention was contentious. The Douglas faction was vilified for appeasing the Abolitionists and Republicans. In spite of his political leanings toward Douglas, and because of his proslavery stance, Candidate Jackson walked a tightrope into his nomination for Governor.

Even though believing in the Breckenridge platform, Jackson and his followers were aware of his lack of national appeal. Somehow, by bobbing and weaving his way through the political landscape, Claiborne Jackson won the prize he had sought. Other proslavery candidates followed him to the state capital in Jefferson City. In Missouri, state elections were held in August while national votes were cast in November.

Jackson was followed into office by Lieutenant Governor Thomas C. Reynolds, a radical pro southern, pro secessionist and incredibly well educated man, conversant in many languages.

There were four candidates for president of the United States in the election of 1860. On the Democratic side in Missouri the contest was between Stephen A. Douglas, John C. Bell and John C. Breckenridge of the southern wing of the Democratic party. Breckenridge was considered the secessionist candidate. Bell was from the Constitutional Unionist party and Douglas carried the traditional torch of the Democratic party: supporting slavery in the existing states, popular sovereignty in the territories while maintaining full allegiance to the Union. In Missouri voters considered both Breckenridge and Lincoln to be too radical. Stephen Douglas squeaked by Bell by less than a percent. Breckenridge, even though a proslavery candidate in a basically pro-slavery state, failed miserably at the polls. And of course, as you know by now, all three candidates fell to Lincoln.

By the elections the historic Whig Party had evolved primarily into the Constitutional Unionist Party. In our neighborhood, the planters were first and foremost businessmen. Though protective of their right to own slaves, they were also political realists. My Pa typified the old ex-Whig philosophy of conservatism. "Do not rock the boat," he had proclaimed on many an occasion.

So the election came and went. Old "Honest Abe" won the national contest but polled only ten percent of the vote in Missouri. Just two counties, St. Louis and Gasconade, both highly populated by German Americans, went with Lincoln.

With Lincoln winning, our elected state officials were in a state of near panic. The majority were Breckenridge holdovers. One Republican senator tried to govern with six Douglas democrats and five Constitution Unionists senators. My Pa said it was "one goddamned hell of a mess!" At any rate, our state was definitely under the control of the secessionists.

To make matters worse, that old St. Louis power broker, Frank Blair, and his cronies had deserted the Democratic Party for the radical Republicans. Blair had developed a long standing friendship with the new president and we could all be sure that he was not about to let this political power go to waste.

*   *   *

Back in Howard County, Durette Henry had mixed emotions. He was greatly disappointed in the election outcome. On the national political front the election of Abraham Lincoln caused him great concern. "What the hell are we going to do?" he asked one day when we were out riding the fences. "This is going to be really bad, Billy. People just don't understand the consequences. Have you been keeping up with the newspapers?"

"Yes, Pa," I said, "but I just don't understand those people out in South Carolina. And to tell you the truth, I'm worried about our neighbors. There's talk about your friend the governor. When I took the eggs into the Fayette Market last week there was a gaggle of men down at the feed store that were talking about him. Old man Holman said that Jackson's parents were pretty smart 'cause when he was born they named him Claiborne F. Jackson and the F. stands for 'Fox'. Holman said he's a fox, all right, that's how he is. All high and mighty up there in the capital. What do you think that's all about, Pa?"

Pa twisted in the saddle and drew up on the reins. I pulled up next to him and we were silent for a moment. Then he spoke:

"Young man, you have always been wiser than your years. Your brothers work hard and have good hearts, but they don't care much for book learning, or politics and such. They are more interested in good horses and pretty women. Nothing wrong with that, they will be fine. And Billy, you are too, but you are a thinker. You love your books. In many ways the row you hoe is gonna be harder than theirs."

I didn't know what to say. I started to respond, but Pa raised his hand and continued,

"Now Billy, you asked about Governor Jackson and I'll give you my opinion, but I want you to keep this just between us. Our friends and neighbors will hear my opinion when I want them to. All right?"

I was interested but a little uncomfortable being party to such a seemingly important discussion. "Sure enough, Pa," I said.

"It's this way son," Durette continued. "Claib sure enough is a fox, I guess all them politicians are. But sometimes you have to do things that go against your personal grain. Politics in general and especially here in our fine state are really complicated. We have those fancy folks in St. Louis and all them goddamned Dutch (actually, they weren't really Dutch. Back then people called our citizens of German origin the name they called themselves, which was Deutch. Only they misheard it and then mispronounced it. And so Dutch they became). And those Republican abolitionists who get all riled up about the Union. The Union! Who gives a damn about those folks? It's what happens here at home that matters. This state, this sovereign state is our home, our concern. It don't have anything to do with Boston or Washington City. They, the Yankees and such, are trying to take what is ours. "It's all about states' rights. That's true in South Carolina; that's true right here in Howard County. You know I voted Whig for years. And then the party sort if fizzled out. Some of us leaned towards the states rights platform, some others sided with James Rollins and his free-soil Whigs. I stuck with George Goode and states rights. This split the party, remember 'divide and conquer,' so we eventually hooked up with John Bell and the Constitutional Unionists. You know how I believed in that man.

I'm a conservative, most of us north of the river are conservative. We don't want to leave the Union, we just want the Union to leave us alone. Slavery works for the large planters. It ain't going to last forever, but for now let's leave well enough alone. Now Mr. Jackson, he is a true aristocrat, just like Mr. Yates and Mr. Thompson. They have a huge investment in their plantations and they need people to farm them. It's business for them, big business. If we didn't have your aunt's slaves, it would hurt, but we could make do, hire some extra help, probably even be more profitable in the long run. But Mr. Jackson would be facing hard times, perhaps even bankruptcy."

We dismounted and perched on a rail fence underneath a large blackjack oak. Pa passed the water jug he carried in his saddle bag, and continued, "That's why Jackson and the others were so involved in supporting Breckenridge. I understand why they are that way, but Breckenridge would bring on secession and mark my words, son, secession will bring on war. Old 'Honest' Abe ain't going to stand for secession, cause he don't give a good god-dammit for States Rights."

"But Pa," I interrupted, "Mr. Jackson ran on the ticket with Stephen Douglas Democrats."

"Yes, Billy, that's why they call him a fox. Jackson, like Vice President Breckenridge, preached that the Federal Government (read Congress) had no right to meddle in the abolishment of slavery. You know this is how President Buchanan feels and it's the same with our former presidents Franklin Pierce and John Tyler. But most of us, like I said, are conservative. We believe that ultimately a fight with the Yankees will lead to the abolition of slavery anyway. That is how we voted. Jackson the Fox knew that Breckenridge's party couldn't win, so he aligned with Mr. Douglas. I think he should have been with me and the Bell supporters, but he played the middle and got himself elected. Of course folks called our Union party the "Do Nothing" Party because we wouldn't take a stand on the slavery issue. Well," he said and paused a long moment. "Enough of this politics talk, Billy. I'm getting all riled up."

We mounted our horses and started for home When we neared the farm Pa said, "And one more thing, Billy. If you learn one thing from our little con-fab let it be this. Mr. Lincoln and his damned Re-publicans could not have won the national election if the rest of us could have come together on a candi-date. As it was, our vote was split and the Yankee lawyer won with less than forty percent of the vote. Remember what I say Billy. Divide and conquer, di-vide and conquer!"

With that proclamation Pa spurred his horse and cantered toward the barn.

Chapter Six

Everyone around these parts was aware that an historic event was looming on the horizon in Jefferson City. Early on the first day of the new year 1861 Jacob loaded the buckboard and carried Pa and me into Fayette. Due to the popularity of the upcoming inauguration all steamboat cabins were booked, so a comfortable ride down river was not an option. Instead, dressed in our finest clothing, we boarded a stage coach and commenced the overland trip to the capitol city.

The old Boonslick Road was filled with local residents headed to celebrate the election of their friend and neighbor. It was a cold but dry day and I was excited and energized. I had never been this far east before and was looking forward to this new adventure. The ancient trail was now a substantial road which had been diverted from its original site to lead directly through the main street, named Broadway, into the thriving town of Columbia. Broadway lived up to its name since it was the widest road I had ever seen. It was one hundred feet wide and, I was told, the scene of some very important horse races. Another passenger pointed out that Columbia had become a major seat of commerce and law in the state.

I had often thought about attending the public university that had been established in 1839, but felt that during these trying times it would be best for me to stay home and help on the farm.

The stage stopped at a tavern on the outskirts of town and we were delighted to stretch our legs and catch a bite to eat. After a couple of hours rest and a change of horses we resumed our places in the coach and headed south to the capitol. We stopped again at Ashland at an inn where we spent the night. It was a crowded and cold place but we made the best of it. Early in the morning we continued our bumpy ride. By midday we boarded a ferry that took us over the wide river and then walked the rest of the way into the city of Jefferson.

January 3, 1861 was relatively mild as hundreds of people arrived to witness the inauguration, and we stood with them as Claiborne Jackson mounted the stage and addressed the throng. The spectators were spellbound as he proclaimed how the northern states were abandoning the Union, not the south. "The south are not aggressors. They only ask to be left alone," he declared.

I poked my father and whispered in his ear "Sounds like we elected Breckenridge." Durette nodded in agreement. Towards the end of the speech Jackson called for a convention to determine how the people of Missouri felt about remaining in the union.

This had become a hot topic since South Carolina had seceded from the union in December of 1860 and word had reached the west that a convention in Delaware had rejected secession.

Our trip home was more comfortable since Pa was able to book passage on a steamboat. No state-rooms were available but since it was just a day trip it didn't matter. I was anxious to get home and tell Miss Millicent and the others, especially Milly, about the inaugural events. It was common knowledge that Milly had a beau, but my sixteen year old hor-mones continued to boil over this remarkable young woman.

By the time the legislature gathered on February 10, a great deal had happened since Jackson's inau-gural address. Mississippi, Alabama, Florida, Geor-gia, Louisiana and Texas had seceded. On February 8 these states and South Carolina had joined to-gether to form a "Confederate" government. As if this was not enough for the delegates to consider, Kansas had been admitted to the Union as a free state.

The legislature called for the election of delegates to meet later in the month to determine the will of the people of Missouri. At the convention the voting revealed that none of the delegates were dyed-in-the-wool secessionists. The unconditional Unionists re-ceived eight out of ten votes.

Former Governor Sterling Price came to the con-vention from his tobacco plantation back in Chariton County. Even though he was the leader of the Constitutional Unionist Party, who favored remaining in the Union, with few exceptions he was popular and was elected President of the gathering. The delegates expressed their discontent with northern leadership's reaction to the secession of the seven states of the Confederacy which could lead to war in the future. However, a resolution was adopted by the convention rejecting secession.

I read the following quote from the Franklin newspaper.

"...At the present, there was no adequate cause to impel Missouri to dissolve her connection with the Federal Union."

I chuckled and pronounced to my family that had gathered to listen to the news, "I'll bet you six bits that old Jackson and Reynolds are going crazy."

Pa said, "I won't bet you 'cause we all know those gents were hoping for secession, especially Reynolds. We also know that if Yankees start shooting at our brothers in the south we had better be oiling up our guns, because most Missourians will go to the ramparts."

I jumped into the breach. "What do you think, Pa? Do you think we had better double our militia drills?" "We will see, son, we will see," he replied.

Double indeed! There was a concerted effort to unify the various county militias into a cohesive military organization. My Howard County unit which had been loosely organized at best, now became officially part of the Missouri State Guard. Hostile emotions were running high but I was apprehensive. I was just about seventeen now and leaning more and more towards the university and studying the law, especially under the pressure exerted by Miss Millicent, who was now our former teacher since she no longer spent winters at the Peyton home. Miss Millicent Yates had recently married the son of a prominent Randolph County planter. Her new husband had been elected to the state senate and had also been elected to serve in the state guard. We were all very happy for the now Mrs. Captain Cecil Patrick Parks. But I missed her dearly. Most of my fellow militia men were chomping at the bit to skin a Yankee, but I remembered the cold stare of the executed men near the Marais des Cygnes and knew it was not that simple a thing to contemplate.

The Jayhawkers were still raising hell, even coming as far as Independence, Waverly and Hickman Mills on their raids. This angered me, but I was also very much aware of the continued retaliation by my fellow Missourians. Would this ever stop, I wondered? Probably not, since things were heating up not only in Missouri but all over the south.

Here is the situation statewide that existed in this critical time.

Governor Jackson and his associates were disappointed that the convention failed to authorize Missouri becoming part of the newly formed southern nation. Contingency plans were enacted, however, because events were occurring at breakneck speed.

Though still officially neutral to secession it became clear to Governor Jackson that if conditions
changed his newly authorized Missouri State Guard
would need arms. The state was surrounded on
three sides by free states. Missouri was a wealthy
state blessed with strategic waterways. St. Louis
was the seat of western commerce and Mr. Lincoln's
friends, the crafty Blair brothers with the damn
Dutch (German American) power block, were a constant cause for concern. If they could be controlled,
the non-foreign citizens of St. Louis, who were mostly
supporters of states rights, would take over. And St.
Louis housed the arsenal crammed full of arms,
ammunition and the tools needed to manufacture
them.

In late January, Governor Jackson cemented his
plan to secure the arsenal when and if the time for
secession ever came. The person appointed to this
task was a West Point graduate who was the present
commander of the State Guard, General Daniel M.
Frost. Frank Blair was also acutely aware of the sig-
nificance of the St. Louis arsenal. He was angered
that his candidate Thomas Hart Benton had been
defeated by Jackson in the recent gubernatorial election. Like Lincoln, he now embraced the Republican
position of limiting slavery to the current slave
states. He was leery of the northern abolitionists
who lobbied with verbiage and guns for slavery's end.
But he was also keenly aware of the competition between the northern mercantile capitalism and the

planters need to expand their agrarian economy in order to compete.

Blair chuckled at his political gatherings, calling Lincoln and his followers "Black Republicans." St. Louis was home for the largest German American population in the states. Following the French Revolution of 1789 Europe experienced decades of war. After Napoleon's defeat in 1815 times were extremely hard for the citizens of the German States. Along with high taxes and crop failures political unrest led to another revolution that attempted to unify the country. By 1848, Many had fled from the failed revolution in their Fatherland, and many of those, some veterans of that conflict, ended up in Missouri. They were skilled in military drill and fiercely loyal to their newly adopted homeland. Quietly, German American athletic clubs had been transforming into paramilitary organizations. Frank Blair's "Wide Awakes" were becoming a formidable force he now named the "Home Guards." All that was needed was for Blair to solidify his position with official support from the United States Army. The current officer in charge, William H. Bell, was a questionable ally.

Spies had reported to Blair the contents of a letter sent to General Frost on January 24, 1861, by Bell assuring him essentially that if push came to shove, Missouri would have the right to claim the arsenal since it was on her soil.

Not surprisingly, Bell was soon relieved by a union leaning officer named Hagner. Blair's solidification of Union strength in St. Louis arrived from Ft. Riley, Kansas, in the person of Captain Nathaniel Lyon and his company of weather-beaten regulars. Originally a Pierce backer, Lyon's experience in the border wars had converted him into a rabid abolitionist who hated everything the pro-slavery Missourians stood for.

Lyon was small in stature and large in personality. Rigid and opinionated, he had not been popular with his fellow officers at Fort Scott and Fort Riley, Kansas. Blair, now a colonel in the competing Missouri Home Guard felt that this fiery redheaded fanatic was just what the doctor ordered to cure the sickness that had infected his home state. Captain Lyon had proven to the pro-slavery settlers on the Kansas prairies that he was a dangerous man and there was no reason to believe that he would not insure equal damage to Blair's enemies here.

Following the inauguration of Abraham Lincoln on March 4th, 1861, Frank Blair orchestrated the transfer of Captain Lyon to the St. Louis arsenal to replace Major Hagner.

The area commander of federal troops, General Harney, was an aristocratic gentleman with many pro-southern friends and like those before him, chose not to rock the boat. Lyon, with no authority over Harney's command, was practically foaming at the mouth, which some of his peers in Kansas said he did literally when cursing the slavers. Blair was his champion, especially since he had persuaded

Secretary of War Simon Cameron (a post previously held by Mr. Jefferson Davis) to direct Lyon to this current cauldron of discontent. What were Blair and Lyon to do?

Governor Jackson and the legislature had orchestrated a coup d'etat giving him authority to select the police chief of St. Louis. The recently elected mayor was also pro secession so southern sympathizers were systematically gaining political control. Only the Blair faction, less than 100 Federal troops and the Dutch stood firm in opposition.

Governor Jackson also had the legal authority to order his Missouri State Militias to organize training camps. All over the state partisans had been drilling in the name of protecting the citizens from any tyranny perpetrated by the federal authorities. In order to enhance their capabilities, the sixty thousand muskets and accompanying powder and cartridges lodged at the arsenal was a tempting target. The problem was that any act of aggression by the state militia would be an illegal traitorous act, and would not be acceptable to the neutrality seeking population of the state, who were in the majority.

However, it would do no harm, Jackson surmised, to establish a training camp in the St. Louis area, because Missouri needed to be prepared. After all, Fort Sumter had fallen to South Carolina militia forces just a month earlier on April 14ᵗ. Therefore, during the first week of May, Governor Jackson ordered General Frost to build a training camp on the western outskirts of St. Louis at a place known as Lindell Grove.

Orders calling for the Howard County Contingent to muster as soon as possible at Franklin had been received. Each Minute Man (as we were often called after those gallant men who had participated in an earlier revolution) was to bring enough food to get them to camp, along with their personal weapons and bedding. Only a few of the officers had any semblance of uniforms but all of us were in high spirits, especially Jacob. Since we would be traveling to St. Louis by steamboat, he was especially excited because this just might be the experience that would cut his ties with the farm and send him on a new career path as a sailor. He would see what happened at Lindell Grove, and then move on from there.

Early in the morning of May 4th the militia mustered all who were able to attend. Jacob and I represented the Peyton obligation since the duties of running the farm during the spring season demanded that Pa, George William and Guffey stay there.

General Frost of the Missouri State Militia had graduated from the United States Military Academy three years later than his soon to be antagonist, Nathaniel Lyon. He had not remained on active duty, instead choosing a life in politics and serving as a Missouri state senator.

Lindell Grove was an ideal location for a training camp since it was near the city. Frost named the camp after Governor Jackson and the smartly aligned streets were given names for prominent Confederate leaders. It was no mystery as to where his allegiance rested.

Meanwhile in the city, similar flurries of activity were occurring. Another West Point man, Lieutenant John Schofield, was commissioned to recruit volunteers for the Union. The department commander refrained from arming them, however.

This did not present much of a problem for long. General Harney decided to travel east to confer with higher authorities regarding the smoldering situation along the banks of the Mississippi River. The old cliché "when the cat's away, the mice will play" came to reality in St. Louis.

Captain Nathaniel Lyon and Colonel Frank Blair swiftly took control. Lyon had the arsenal emptied, its contents sent to safety in Illinois. The volunteer regiments under Colonels Blair, Boerenstein and Sigel were mustered into United States service. Heinrich Boerenstein and Franz Sigel had been instrumental in the development and training of the German units.

Sigel, a small bespectacled teacher of mathematics and history at the German American Institute was rumored to have been a commanding general on the losing side during the European Revolution back in 1848. Along with the news of the establishment of Camp Jackson, Lyon discovered that a shipment of mortars had arrived on the St. Louis docks disguised as crates of marble.

By the time we had settled into the daily routine of camp life, unbeknownst to us, Lyon, Blair and company had assembled and drilled 6,500 armed troops.

General Frost continued to drill the 891 men under his command, having no idea that a large threat loomed on the eastern horizon.

I'm sure it must have been difficult for professional military men to swallow how a relatively low ranking officer like Captain Lyon could wield so much power. Suffice it to say that Frank and Montgomery Blair had the president's ear and under the threat of losing Missouri to the Confederacy, they had been given free reign to act with impunity as they changed the course of history.

With General Harney, the commander of the United States Military Department of the west, out of the way in Washington, oblivious to the Blair brothers work towards deposing him, Captain Lyon reigned supreme.

Meanwhile the unsuspecting Missouri State Militia, including these two farm boys, continued to enjoy our time away from our ordinary lives of farming and shop keeping. General Frost had heard rumors, however, and was preparing a note to Lyon asking if the rumors of his intention of attacking the camp were true.

Jacob and I and some others were talking outside our four-man tent after a filling if not very tasty meal of cornbread and beans, flavored with a ham hock or two.

The camp was alive with the news that Arkansas had seceded from the Union on that very day, May 6, 1861, and it sparked several conversations about our own situation.

One of the boys from a plantation in Boone County raised the question that was on all our minds. "There's lots of talk about if we'ens is going to go into town and take that Yankee arsenal. What do you all think?"

Jacob said, "No, it ain't going to happen. We are here to show a force. Ain't nobody wants war. We don't want to secede. We like things just the way they is. All we, well, all I want is to be left alone. I'm for States Rights. If we have to free our colored folks, that's just fine with me. They is family and they will stay and work with us anyway."

I said, "That's true with our Negroes, but I don't think our old friend Governor Jackson would feel that way."

Jacob said, "Well to hell with that old sonofabitch, he ain't got nothing to do with me."

"Oh, I'm afraid he does," chimed in another tent mate. Look at where we are. If them lop-eared Dutch want us, they will come to get us. I don't know about you, but I'd keep my powder dry and close and sleep with one eye open."

I said, "I'm not so sure about that. I think this whole thing will be over soon. Remember, nothing happened during that commotion back in April." "Which commotion? Jacob asked. "There have been so many."

"The mob taking the arsenal back at Liberty, you dummy," I went on. "The Mayor of St. Joseph, Mr. Jeff Thompson, remember, Jacob, we saw him when we were out at the border a couple of years ago. He and some others raised several battalions. I tell you the Yankees know they stuck a stick in a hornet's nest. They got their hands full with the new Confederate states. They got stung at Fort Sumter. They ain't going to bother with us."

"Yep," the Randolph County volunteer added, "and now they got Arkansas to worry about."

But Captain Lyon was not thinking about Arkansas. With the advent of Camp Jackson and the confiscation of the clandestine mortars, Captain Lyon was beside himself. Spies kept him regularly informed as to the activities of Frost's troops and Lyon was bound and determined to put a stop to the Missouri State Guard. The only problem was that he had no authority to act. Any military action would be an unlawful act of aggression. He was a relatively small frog in a very large pond. After all, General Harney was still the man in charge. The answer to Lyon's dilemma would have to come from the Blair brothers and the nation's president.

Back in April, at the urging of the Blairs, the president had executed an order relieving Harney of his duties – to be delivered when or if needed. Harney was oblivious to this conspiracy and continued to seek guidance from his military superiors out east.

By April 9th, Lyon could stand the situation no longer. A council of Unionists was gathered at the captain's request, but the lawyers disappointed Lyon by reminding him that the flag of the United States fluttered above the tents of Lindell Grove and that the militia gathering was entirely legal. In no uncertain terms Lyon was told that the Missouri State Militia had every legal right to meet and drill as they saw fit. This did not satisfy the spunky little captain, and he continued to scheme.

At Camp Jackson, May 10th started just like the other days at the bivouac. Breakfast, inspection, and drill occupied the morning. Following the lunch break the militia men dusted their weapons and took a little personal time.

About three in the afternoon nature struck me with a vengeful call and I headed off at full speed to the outhouses which were located at some distance and down wind from the living area of the camp. These "two holers," as they were fondly called, were hastily constructed outhouses located over a shallow pit. Buckets of lime were provided to cover the excrement and shredded copies of the St. Louis Enquirer added a modicum of comfort.

Jacob laughed as I ran to the latrines but figured he might as well join me. He lit his corncob pipe which not only perked him up but helped mask the smell emanating from these foul necessities. Suddenly there was a great commotion in the camp. Jacob saw the horizon filling with blue coated figures and, instinctively, he knew that the glint of sunlight from hundreds of bayonets did not bode well for the Missouri State Militia.

"Billy, Billy," Jacob yelled as he pounded on the flimsy door, "Get out here, now!" Pulling up my britches I leaped from the structure and yelled back "What, what's going on?" And then I saw the cause of Jacob's distress. "Get the hell out of here," I said, and we started to run.

Others who had seen the advance of the Union troops were heading for the woods and weeds as fast as their feet could take them. We followed in hot pursuit. Everyone ran for about a quarter of a mile and we dove into a shallow gully to catch our breaths and see what was going on. Some of the others just kept on going. One of our Howard County neighbors who had been carrying water from the creek outside the camp came running by. "Where are you going?" I cried.

He kept running but shouted as he crashed through the weeds, "I'm going home. They's going to kill us," and on he went.

Jacob, still out of breath, started to laugh in spite of the seriousness of the situation. "Did you see that?" he said, "He's still carrying that water bucket!"

Earlier that day, Captain Lyon had executed his plan on no authority but his own. In all, 6,500 troops, mostly the damn Dutch volunteers, were dispersed into four separate columns and proudly marched through the St. Louis streets. A huge crowd followed the would-be warriors. The rumors of an attack on Camp Jackson were coming true.

The hostile captain rode at the head of his two companies of regulars. Laclede Avenue, Pine, Olive and Market streets were filled with the sound of footsteps from the smartly dressed German American troops. The commotion increased as even more curious citizens followed the formations toward Lindell Grove.

Two graduates of the West Point Military Academy found themselves caught up in the crowd. Neither knew of the important role they would play in the years to come. Ulysses S. Grant had returned to the army after several unsuccessful attempts at business and was currently posted as a recruiting officer in Illinois. He just happened to be visiting St. Louis on that fateful day.

Unknown to Grant, another spectator and former Army officer, William Tecumseh Sherman was following the throng. After his army commitment he had practiced law in Lawrence, Kansas, but was currently employed as the president of a St. Louis street car company.

Due to my upset bowel and Jacob's eagle eye we, along with a couple hundred others, were able to escape the snare. General Frost was incredulous that the scrappy captain had the nerve to execute such a daring and illegal action against his surprised, confused and greatly outnumbered State Guard.

After surrounding Camp Jackson, Lyon demanded the Militias surrender. Our boys were accused of hostility toward the federal Government and intending to overthrow it as well. We learned all this later in one of the longest days I had ever spent.

Chapter Seven

So there we were. Frost protested, but to no avail. In all, 689 men out of the 891 who had mustered that morning were rounded up and marched to captivity in the city.

Although we only heard about it later, we took some small solace in the fact that Lyon and Siegal were robbed of a little dignity and unable to fully savor their victory due to a couple of freak accidents.

Upon receiving news of Frost's surrender, the triumphant Lyon dismounted and was promptly kicked in the stomach by an aide's horse. The second most important figure in this episode of Missouri history, Colonel Franz Sigel, was injured when his horse slipped on the pavement.

In spite of his injury, Lyon issued orders, and the disarmed prisoners were herded toward the arsenal. As the Missouri State Guard proceeded east the civilian crowd became increasingly hostile.

The crowd shouted "Damn the Dutch!" and other slurs. Disturbances broke out among the bystanders. A shot rang out wounding one of the German soldiers. Like the "shot heard around the world" which ignited the Revolutionary War, this act by an intoxicated partisan sparked a bloody reprisal. Colonel Boernstein ordered his troops to return fire. Chaos reigned and in the end, twenty eight civilians were killed and seventy five wounded. The pro-southern citizens were outraged. The "Damn Dutch" had not only killed civilians, but two of the victims were women and one was a babe in arms.

Gaining a little courage and not knowing what else to do we followed the mob into town. Besides the shock of the attack and capture of our friends and companions, it was dawning on us that we were now utterly on our own. We had the clothes on our back and nothing more. We had lost our guns and personal belongings back at camp. The reality of our situation was sinking in. I guessed we would be considered fugitives.

After the prisoners were gone, the crowd eventually dispersed. Outside a tavern on Market Street a crowd of angry young obviously pro-southern men had gathered.

I took a chance and approached one of the older, but equally vocal, supporters. Cautiously, I relayed our story. Much to my surprise we instantly assumed the status of heroes. I didn't feel much like a hero, in fact I was starting to feel profound guilt at having escaped, leaving my companions to experience captivity and an unknown future. But the tavern crowd felt differently. A collection was quickly taken and suddenly we were back on our feet.

Our generous fans provided beer and food in that order and mustered up enough cash to allow us to put up at an inn and to purchase steamboat passage home. On our way toward cheap lodging near the levee key we passed through the notorious red light district. We had heard stories about painted ladies standing under the gas lights but now we actually saw them. Jacob had consumed a few more lagers than I, and started to respond to the beckoning belles, but I steered him quickly by even if we were a little wobbly. It was not that we had not tasted beer and whiskey before, but never in the quantity that the celebration of our freedom had brought about.

The inn we found provided a reasonably safe, if crowded, room filled with sour smelling, snoring men but the alcohol quickly brought about sleep. The next morning weighed heavy on us as our heads pounded and throbbed like the thunder of a roaring steam engine.

The word on the street regarding the Camp Jackson Militia was that they were not being paroled. This bothered me a great deal, especially since we were free and the outlook of our comrades in arms was extremely problematic. We talked about how the federal Dutch had taken such an unfair advantage of the militia and we vowed to avenge the injustice of it all.

The angry mood had prevailed throughout the night and into the morning. The mayor had even ordered the saloons closed, but unfortunately not before we experienced the damages. We heard that ex-governor and Chariton County neighbor Sterling Price had spoken to an angry crowd gathered in front of the Planters House Hotel. Prior to taking the train to the capital city he had denounced Lyon's actions labeling them "military despotism."

As we hungover fugitives loitered outside the steamboat office, Jacob witnessed a life changing exchange between a weathered seaman and a pompous German clerk. It seemed that new rules were in place requiring all steamboat pilots who wished to be licensed to take an oath of allegiance to the United States of America.

Voices were raised as the American pilots argued and cursed the newly arrived German officials. The vocal man was a veteran pilot by the name of Absalom Grimes. "I don't object to no oath," he said, "my father and grandfather were Americans, but I'll be damned if I'll take the oath from a Dutchman who can hardly talk English," he pronounced to the assembled multitude.

Some of the young men who were with Grimes continued to complain about the injustice foisted upon the pilots. One disgruntled pilot grumbled, "I ain't going to tote no damned Dutch anywhere!"

Jacob had stuck up a conversation with another young man who had traveled to St. Louis seeking a pilot's license. It had been a long time dream of Jacob's to work on the river and he was thrilled to talk to someone who had experienced the life. The two hit it off from the start and Jacob was mesmerized by the stories heard from his new friend. I was still nursing a brain splitting headache and simply wanted the boat to shove off so I could go home and close this painful chapter of my young life.

The steamboat was scheduled to leave soon and I announced that we should board before long. "Billy," Jacob said as he pulled me aside, "it's now or never. I'm not going home with you. Sam said he could get me a job and if I paid attention and studied up, I could be a pilot. Don't look at me that way, Billy. This is what I have always wanted. Tell Ma and the family that I'll write them soon as I get settled."

I was shocked. "Are you insane?" I blurted.

Jacob said "Don't do this to me. You know this is what I have always wanted."

"Yes, yes, yes," I know, I said. "Damn it all, it's just so sudden."

Jacob pleaded "Your Pa always says strike while the iron is hot, and the iron is hot now!"

On the one hand I could see Jacob's point of view. After all, he had also tasted the thrill of adventure. On the other hand, this was certainly a wild hair. I had no way of knowing I would never see my cousin and best friend again.

And so it went. Jacob redeemed his ticket and stood on the levee until the steamboat, with me aboard, slipped out of sight. True to his word, Jacob sent us letters outlining his adventures. After my departure we learned he purchased a new ticket for a trip up the Mississippi with his new friends. A native of Hannibal, Missouri, Jacob's new friend Sam Clemens found him a job there as a stevedore and lodgings in a small room over a hardware store. This was a far cry from the relative luxury he had experienced on the Peyton farm but he thrived in his new found freedom.

It seems that not long after settling in Hannibal he was rounded up with Sam and some other pilots by a squad of Union soldiers who took them back to St. Louis to ferry troops on the Missouri River. But they outfoxed the Yankees and no sooner than they arrived they slipped away and found their way back to the Hannibal wharf.

Happy to be back in Hannibal and away from the hated Federals, they settled down to business as usual. This didn't last long, however, since they decided to join the local Missouri State militia, known as the Ralls County Rangers. I'd thought that Jacob would have had enough of the military because of our disastrous Camp Jackson experience, but I guess not.

The regimental commander established this unit for the sole purpose of defending the area from the St. Louis Germans. Life in the Rangers seemed to agree with Jacob, Sam and their companions. They were not well armed. Jacob said his only weapon was a keenly sharpened corn knife, but the wealthy planters provided them with the finest rations available. I've heard it said that "an army travels on its stomach," and Jacob always had a hungry stomach.

In his most recent letter Jacob pondered the current turn of events. He had wanted to travel the rivers but had ended up again in the militia. "Life is hard to understand," he had opined. His friend Sam had told him that the current state of affairs wouldn't last long and that they would be back on the river soon.

Jacob was looking forward to a trip down river to New Orleans. I could just about picture that far away look he always got when he spoke of potential river travel.

There was a great deal of rejoicing by my family upon my safe return. Everyone had assumed the worst and feared for my health and safety if imprisoned. Jacob's Ma and my cousins were relieved that he was safe and out of harm's way on the river.

Neighbors dropped by to hear about my adventures at Camp Jackson, from the horse's mouth, they said.

In gripping detail I told of all I had seen and heard. I did neglect to elaborate about how I had been scared shitless, literally, and of course leaving out the night of debauchery and the next morning's retribution.

Meanwhile, down in Jefferson City, as you might imagine, the politicians were struggling with the aftermath of the fall of Camp Jackson. Missourians who had previously supported the Union were now up in arms over the brash actions of Lyon and his damned Dutch cohorts. The question on everyone's mind was "What would Lyon do next?"

The answer came swiftly and soon. Shortly after the fall of our militia camp and the massacre, General Harney returned to the chaos in St. Louis. Captain Lyon had over stepped his authority for sure, but the power brokers in Washington City had done nothing to stop him. This is when Frank Blair played his trump card, and served the orders he had been carrying relieving Harney of his duties. In a single blow Harney was out and the fanatical Captain Lyon was jumped four pay grades to Brigadier General. To be fair, Blair had received word that Confederate sympathizers like St. Joseph Mayor Thompson and General Rains were actively recruiting along our western border, so he needed a strong leader pronto! He made the only move he deemed open to him.

The government in Jefferson City was in a panic. They quickly passed a military bill formally installing the Missouri State Guard as the state's army. Railroads and telegraphs were nationalized and Sterling Price was dispatched to confer with the United States Army commander of the west, who on the 30th of May had become the newly minted brigadier.

While he was in charge, General Harney had been more conciliatory to the state officials than the cheeky Lyon and had agreed on peaceful terms with Price. Under that agreement, Federal troops would remain in St. Louis but would be withdrawn from

Jefferson City. This meant that the crisis would be averted as Missouri would remain neutral. I have come to believe that it does no good to speculate on "what ifs?" even though historians always do so. But I will speculate and say that if the Harney-Pierce agreement had been honored by the Lincoln administration, Missouri would have remained a neutral state instead of ending up as what the Yankee president later called "a killing field."

Loyal pro-union, pro-slavery Missourians like Squire Yates were pressing our leaders for a reasonable and peaceful solution. Under a flag of truce, Claiborne Jackson, the duly elected governor of the state, Thomas L. Snead, his secretary, and the former governor and current commander of the Missouri State Guard, General Sterling Price, met with Frank Blair, Jr., Nathanial Lyon and his secretary Horace Conant at the Planter's House in downtown St. Louis.

It was the 10th of June when the opposing forces faced each other. The state delegation, for their part, was conciliatory. Jackson basically offered the same terms as the earlier agreement if Lyon would send his volunteer troops home and not occupy the state.

But Blair could not condone State's Rights, especially since the Republicans were in control of the federal government. Lyon was even more solidified by his hatred of Missourians in general.

After hours of Blair preaching the Republican agenda in the stifling heat, Lyon could contain himself no longer. In words that would affect the lives of all citizens of the state for generations to come, the Connecticut Yankee took command and spoke these fateful words:

"Rather than concede to the State of Missouri the right to demand that my government shall not enlist troops within her limits, or bring troops into the state whenever it please, or move its troops at its own will into, or out of, or through the state; rather than concede to the State of Missouri for one single instant the right to dictate to my government in any matter, however unimportant, I would rather see you, and you, and you and you, and you, and every man, woman, and child in the state, dead and buried."

This diatribe was dutifully recorded by both scribes in the room. Before he marched from the room, with spurs and saber jangling, Lyon turned his eyes on Governor Jackson and coldly said. "This means war!" He then dismissed our Jefferson City contingent who rushed back to share the news with nervous legislators, stopping only to burn railroad bridges and cut the telegraph wires. They took him at his word.

Our depleted Fayette militia, now officially part of the State Guard, was put on alert. A group from Randolph County had already gathered and was waiting for arms that Jackson's supporters had promised them. The citizens of Howard County and a significant number of men from the western border region were beside themselves upon hearing the latest news.

"How in hell can that one little sonofabitch make a declaration of war on the sovereign State of Missouri?" my Pa yelled. We were all angry and humiliated regarding the current state of affairs. Our state government was in shambles under the boot of the pursuing federal zealots and Frank Blair's home guards now felt they held the upper hand as they became more aggressive by the hour.

It was unusual for Pa to go on like he was, but his ranting continued, "These damn Dutch are feeling their oats, and it simply don't bode well with me. It's not safe for any of us. I got word that there are hostile federals stalking about."

Squire Yates and his new son-in-law were gathered in our front yard under the shade of the ancient maple tree.

Yates continued the conversation, "I have heard how up near Lexington there have been outright assassinations. Those Yankee lovers are bullying and insulting planters, making threats. They are doing all they can to drive us away or worse. Durette, you know I never wanted us to join the Confederates. I supported the Union. My ancestors, hell, your ancestors fought old King George. We are Union men. But for the love of God, first Camp Jackson, who knows what's next. This new policy of the federal government is rapidly bringing on a conversion experience for me."

Pa interjected, "Squire, what do you think? Will those jackasses out in Washington City allow Lyon's Dutch to continue trampling our privileges and rights with impunity?" I wondered too. I left my elders, saddled up Calico and headed for Fayette to see what our Guard was up to.

Back in April, after the Confederate batteries had fired on Fort Sumter the newly inaugurated president of the United States had called for seventy five thousand volunteers. Governor Jackson had refused to send a single man, believing that the request among other things, was illegal. After meeting with Lyon, he took time out from packing to leave the capitol to issue a call for fifty thousand men from the county militias to muster at Lexington and Boonville as a united force to protect the state from imminent federal invasion. This was on the 12th of June. I thought that this must be an overreaction. Surely the federal government would not invade a sovereign state. This was blatantly against the law of the land. We had not seceded!

But I'll be damned if Lyon and 17,000 troops weren't headed to Jefferson City on steamboats. This invasion prompted our legally elected officials, as many state records as could be hurriedly gathered and the great seal of the state to board the steamboat White Cloud and skedaddle up river. Soon after, Lyon arrived in Jefferson City and met no resistance. Following an overnight stay the conqueror raced on toward Boonville. On June 17th, 1861 the

Missouri River bottoms echoed with the sound of gunfire.

On April 13th, 1861, Union forces had surrendered at Forts Sumter and Moultrie in Charleston Harbor six days following the secession of South Carolina. The next hostile action, this time initiated by the Union, was the capture of the Missouri State Guard on May 10th. On May 24th Colonel Elmer Ellsworth of the 11th New York Infantry was murdered by a southern sympathizer while marching his troops through Baltimore. He became the Union's first martyr. The battle of Philippi was fought in Western Virginia on June 3rd, followed by the battle of Big Bethel, Virginia on June 10th.

Then, on June 17th, we had the first bloody encounter between Brigadier General Lyon and the forces of Major General Price, when Union forces attacked across the Missouri River bottoms towards the bluff near Boonville where the Missouri forces had taken a stand. General Price was absent from the fray due to a case of dysentery. Governor Jackson's nephew, West Point-trained Colonel John Marmaduke was left in charge of the outnumbered, poorly trained and inadequately armed Missouri farm boys.

General Lyon's Germans had the advantage of the training they received in their gymnastic societies and political clubs. Many had served in the revolutionary military in Germany a decade before and all were riled at the anti immigration campaigns that had been waged against them by Ned Buntline and his followers. Lyon's trusty Fort Riley veterans were there along with a cannon and regulars who knew how to use it.

The fight lasted twenty minutes. Marmaduke suffered three men dead and 25 wounded. The Blair-Lyon force lost two to death, nine wounded and one missing.

The good citizens of Boonville surrendered as the State Guard retreated overland toward the south-western part of the state intending to hook up with the forces of Confederate General Ben McCulloch. This withdrawal meant that our rivers and railroads were under the control of federal forces. In spite of our setback that some wags called "the Boonville Races," our boys were still itching for a fight.

Lieutenant Governor Reynolds had struck off to Richmond, Virginia, with a delegation urging the new Confederate President, Jefferson Davis, to provide military support. Davis seemed to be concerned re-garding the legality of this kind of a transaction, le-gality not being much of a concern for the Yankees (I feel moved to point out). Davis procrastinated even though the Confederacy needed all the allies they could muster. My grandmother used to spin the cli-ché "He who hesitates is lost," and that surely was the case here. The swift blue tide now controlled the state's infrastructures and some of our State Guard was holed up near Indian country in the little town of Cowskin Prairie. The occupiers had illegally installed

Hamilton Gamble as Governor with a new pro-Union legislature in Jefferson City. Missouri now had two governments, the legally elected one and the one imposed by the Federals. Gamble didn't want to rock the boat too much, hoping to limit the military action in our state. Against the wishes of the Abolitionists, he issued a statement protecting slavery. It did little to settle the waters.

By late August, recruiting for our cause was at a fevered pitch so General Fremont placed Missouri under martial law. This meant that if we were not given permission from the Federals to carry a gun, we would be shot. Also, in spite of the Governor's statement, slaves, or at least slaves of Confederate sympathizers, would be freed. Who the hell knew where they would go! One good thing that old, crafty Lincoln did was to rescind Fremont's order. Gamble and Lincoln didn't want to lose the border states so they threw us this crumb.

Lyon, unable to pursue by steamboat and lacking adequate supply trains for an overland campaign, left us alone for the moment. I guess he was willing to bide his time and fight another day.

The news about Jefferson City and Boonville spread like a prairie fire. The newly constituted guard from Randolph and Howard Counties was galvanized into action. There were 123 of us between the ages of 17 and 30. I was still the youngest. We were armed and ready to defend our state's rights. Well, we weren't exactly well armed since only about

half of us had weapons and most of these were shotguns and squirrel rifles, no match for the Spring-
fields the Union forces proudly carried. I had nothing to contribute since my beloved rifle had been lost
at Camp Jackson. Pa did give me his prized .45 caliber Philadelphia Derringer which would provide me
with some up close and personal protection, but it
wasn't much to carry into war.

The captain of our volunteers had been told that
arms captured from the Lexington armory would be
waiting for us when we caught up with the main
army.

Our defeat at Boonville was what still stuck in my
craw. I was primed and ready to defend my homeland. I wanted to exact revenge for our humiliation
at the Camp Jackson affair. But I had been raised to
be a peaceful man, and I still had a vivid memory of
the horror near the bank of the Marais des Cygnes.

Honestly, I didn't want to die either, but there
was no way I would let myself be labeled a coward.
Besides, others might catch a Yankee bullet, but I
was sure it wouldn't be me. This was, I guess, the
optimism of youth.

Captain Park, my tutor's new husband, had persuaded me to join the march. Pa had been hesitant
at first, maintaining that I was still young and that
there was plenty of work to be done on the farm.
But the gallant captain eventually wore my folks
down, again saying that they guessed I could go
while Guffey and George William stayed at home to

carry the load once more.

Guffey didn't mind one bit since he was never as adventurous as I was and George was a homebody. The Union supporting press had a field day reporting on the battle of Boonville. One famous political cartoon depicted Governor Jackson dressed in women's clothing and General Price fleeing from a lion with the face of General Lyon. The caption read: "The Battle of Booneville, or the Great Missouri Lyon Hunt."

As we trudged south through Tipton, Cole Camp and Warsaw we felt the sting of this humiliating defeat but we were resolved to redeem our reputations, especially after we were properly trained and armed.

One day as we rested, my friend Willy Williams and I got to talking about our current situation. He lived in Franklin where his father owned a hemp shipping operation and I had known him as long as I could remember.

"Billy," he opined," I don't think the good Lord really wants me to, as you say, 'join the cause.'" He took a breath and continued, "Not much has changed, really. Like everybody here, I can't stand them god damned Dutch and I hope that sonofabitch Lyon gets a bullet through his black heart, but I don't think the federal government will stand for what he did. They got to know it was illegal. I still think we can remain neutral if everybody will just calm down. I don't want us to secede, I just want us to drive them feds back to their homes so they'll leave us alone!"

I said, "Well, Willy, you picked one hell of a time to come up with your decision. We are going to war, boy!"

Chapter Eight

Following the foray at Boonville General Lyon set to work assembling the equipment of war he would need to finish off this upstart rebellion. Ammunition, foodstuffs, horses, mules and wagons with teamsters to drive them had to be gathered. Quartermasters worked feverishly procuring supplies for this overland campaign.

As we made our way southwest, Federal troops were dispatched up river to secure river crossings and to contain the pro-southern forces assembled near Lexington. In Kansas, Union troops were heading south along the borders hoping to engage Jackson's ragged force. Colonel Franz Sigel and 2,000 men were also racing toward the southwestern border intending to squeeze the Governor's band into submission. On July 5th Sigel's wish came true a few miles north of Carthage. But, to the Colonel's surprise, Jackson's ragged and poorly armed men soundly defeated the presumptuous German and his troops. News of Sigel's rout energized the troops and instilled a new sense of pride in the states rights citizens of Missouri.

Folks said that this fight was the first major engagement in this war, since the first battle of Manassas Junction out east in Virginia was to come a couple of weeks later. As with Carthage, we won that battle that the federals called "Bull run."

On the road ahead of us at Springfield lay Lyon with 5,600 men. Fortunately for our guard, he felt outnumbered. He had requested reinforcements from the new Army commander Major General George B. McClellan. Upon learning that nothing would be done regarding his request and acting on his own initiative, without bothering to inform his masters in Washington City, he moved the force he called the "Army of the West" twelve miles south where he surprised the combined armies of the Missouri State Guard under Price and the Confederate force commanded by McCulloch that had recently arrived from Arkansas.

Our Randolph County Rangers had finally met up with the main army at Cowskin Prairie down in the southwestern part of the state. But no sooner had we settled in when the call came down to muster up and head back towards Springfield. By the evening of August 9th we were camped among a grove of oak trees near a stream called Wilson Creek. It had been a miserable evening since it was raining and most of us were soaked and muddy. Even though we faced the prospect of a battle at Springfield our spirits were not as damp as our clothing. None of the leaders had bothered to set pickets and we felt secure as we tended the fires and slept under some new tents the quartermasters had given us.

We had no idea that we would be attacked. The plan was that we would be doing the attacking. I guess Lyon didn't care much for our plan. Colonel Sigel and his cannon were there and he had strategically placed them to the south of our camp. Lyon was to come from the other direction and catch us in a fatal trap, which he damn near did. I was caught off guard and just about jumped out of my drawers when a cannon ball came bouncing into the middle of our camp. I didn't have anything to fight with so I ran into a cornfield and then up to the yard of a house that was situated on a small hill. Smoke, dust and the roar of cannon and gunfire gave me a glimpse into what hell must look like. Men were bringing the wounded up to the house, so I figured I could be of some use in that way. I had never seen anything like this before but after throwing up a couple of times I was able to lend a hand as a poorly equipped nurse.

After six hours of desperate fighting, that "brave" Colonel Sigel just up and left and headed back to Springfield all on his lonesome. Lyon had valiantly rallied his forces on what would come to be called "Bloody Hill," waving his hat and yelling encouragement, but that didn't last long. His horse was shot out from under him and he was wounded in the leg and head. Fearlessly, he had mounted another horse when he met his maker from a musket ball in the chest. As he died his last words were "I fear the day is lost." As much as it pains me to say it, the man did have grit! But his dying words were correct; the day was lost for the Union.

Running out of water, ammunition and will, the now ranking Major Samuel Sturgis ordered his battered survivors to quit the field of battle and the army straggled back to Springfield, leaving the battered body of their late commander crumpled in the blood and dust. Along with Lyon, 1,216 other Union soldiers perished. Five thousand, four hundred men had joined the foray early that August morning. The Confederates and Missouri State Guard had fielded 10,200 men of which 1,230 lost their lives. It was a terrible bloody day for all concerned but the Battle of Oak Hills, that the Yankees called Wilson Creek, was a decided victory for the states rights cause. The newspapers called it a draw, but we knew better. Partisans exuberantly celebrated this victory and those of us who survived the onslaught were especially thankful. I was covered in blood, but none of it was mine. The horror of the Marais des Cygnes had been brutally replaced by an even greater one.

I felt as if I really hadn't helped with the battle, but the surgeons complimented me on my work. I learned a great deal that day, but foremost I learned I did not want to serve in the Medical Corps.

The disgrace of the "Boonville Races" was vindicated. The future of Missouri now looked much brighter. The celebration victory was dampened for some by the reality of the horror of the dead and wounded, but even the families of those soldiers felt pride among their sorrows for the sacrifices their sons and husbands had made for freedom from the oppressors.

The mood in Boone's Lick was euphoric. Hope was indeed springing eternal. "Now that that crazy fool Lyon was dead and the damned lop-eared Dutch defeated, maybe Missouri would be left alone. "Let the Yankee settlers squat in Kansas," Ma spouted off to no one in particular.

The only personally sad part of the Wilson Creek affair for me was the devastating discovery that Captain Cecil Park had been severely wounded by a cannon ball that shattered his leg. Surgeons believed he could be saved and the leg was amputated, but infection set in and he suffered greatly. I wrote a letter he dictated to his wife and family and I eased his pain as much as I could. One of the surgeons gave me a vial of laudanum which helped some. It was a sad scene as delirium took over, but mercifully he died soon after. I knew Miss Millicent and all the Squire's family would be devastated by this loss. Captain Park had dutifully drilled with his militia unit and had willingly ridden with his Randolph County Rangers to the end.

I knew I couldn't remain upset over this man's untimely demise. At times I thought that maybe it had been the will of God that I stay home and help out on the farm. Was I going against that will and would I be further punished for it? I still harbored none of the deep hate for the Union soldiers that my friends did. I had read enough military history as well as having experienced a taste of it myself that I suspected no good could come of this fight. As I walked the battlefield both sides seemed equal in death. I was sad and angry over the death of Captain Park and others in my unit, but it had become clear to me that this was the price of patriotism. Adding to my stress was my continuing fear of being branded a coward. I knew this wasn't true, but I also knew I had experienced the bitter metallic taste of fear.

The battle did provide us with our choice of weapons. A detail had combed the area collecting weapons and we were given our pick. I chose a standard Parker-Hale 1853 3-band .577 caliber Enfield musket. Feeling very much the carrion-picker, I had earlier removed a pistol from the cold dead hand of a federal officer of the First Iowa Volunteers. It was a beautiful steel-framed .36 caliber Navy Colt with ivory grips.

Following the Oak Hill battle, Colonel Franz Sigel, in spite of his poor showing, was placed in charge of the crippled Union army as they made their way northeast towards the railhead at Rolla some sixty miles away.

After the victory, our forces separated, with General McCulloch's boys heading back to Arkansas and our state guard moving out to Springfield and beyond. General Price and the governor had their sightes set on the 3,500 man garrison located on the Missouri River at Lexington, so off we went on August 12th. The weather was nice for this time of year in Missouri and we eventually arrived at our objective a month later on September 13th.

Arriving at Warrensburg on the 11th we were fed a hot meal and given time to clean our weapons and repair our gear. We had marched on hardtack and fatback for a month and the cornbread and sorghum the local ladies prepared for us was a little bit of heaven. Our ranks had grown on the march with farm boys and shopkeepers joining all along the way. There must have been near 10,000 of us now and it was a sight to behold. At night the light from our campfires could be seen for miles.

At Lexington we learned that the federal commander, Colonel James Mulligan had decided to make a stand. Someone said that he was also bound and determined to hang on to the $900,000 dollars he had stolen from a local bank. Ephram Harman, who had marched with us all the way, except for spending one evening with his Ma in Warrensburg, offered that he guessed that much money was worth fighting for, but I wasn't that sure, after the misery I had witnessed at Wilson Creek.

Ephram continued, "Word has it that Mulligan is fit to be tied. He has begged old General Fremont who is now the head of the whole western department for additional troops. You know, I used to think the world of that man. I read about every one of his exploits out in the far west. Anyway, I heard that the good colonel had pleaded for reinforcements but that Fremont is a slow sonofabitch and as indecisive as hell, which is good for our side, I'd say." Ephram was never at a loss for words, especially with a captive audience. He continued, "He was a great pathfinder and explorer, but it looks as if his dabbling in politics has made him soft and way too cautious."

I responded, "Well, happy days for us!" I also heard that Mulligan was seeking assistance from the Jayhawkers but that old bastard Jim Lane was too busy marauding down near our old stomping grounds at Harrisonville to be bothered to respond.

By the 14th of September our number had doubled to over 20,000. I had never seen so many folks all crammed together and I might add I had never smelled a stench that terrible. It seemed that there was no place to go to escape the smell of shit. Horse shit, mule shit, cow shit, and the shit from thousands of poorly fed Missourians was almost more than I could stand. I prayed that Lexington's stubborn Union defenders would be as sick of the smell as I was and raise the white flag. But of course, that was too simple.

I had been assigned to the second division of the Missouri State Guard, under the leadership of General Thomas Harris. There was a steady fire from both sides, but the Yanks weren't budging and we weren't inclined to march across an open field of fire. Events heated up on the 18ᵗʰ of September, I guess you could call that the official start of the battle. For a day or two we had one hell of an artillery battle. We pushed the Federals back to their fortifications around the Masonic College but they hurt our boys in a fight over the Anderson House which was being used as a hospital. Mulligan's garrison was composed of 3,500 men mostly from his 23ʳᵈ Illinois known as the "Irish Brigade," due, I suppose, to the ethnic nature of the volunteers. They were a tough lot, I'll say that for them. I wasn't involved in any of the shooting. Instead, someone came up with an ingenious plan and I was assigned to help implement it. On September 20ᵗʰ we raided a local warehouse full of hemp bales. We soaked them with water and pushed them ahead of us. These mobile breastworks allowed us to creep closer and closer to our enemy. Cannon balls would just bounce off and bullets would simply stick several inches inside the bales.

This was great fun for our boys and relatively safe work. I guess the Colonel had performed the best he could under the circumstances. Outmanned, low on food, water and ammunition, and outsmarted by the use of the hemp bales, Mulligan asked for the terms of surrender late in the afternoon. The concussion caused by the artillery battle had shattered every windowpane in town. The Union soldiers were a thirsty lot as they marched out of their entrenchments and stacked arms. No army, regardless of how well trained and ready to fight, can exist without water.

As things go, casualties were light. We lost twenty-five men killed and seventy-two wounded. The Federals had thirty-nine killed and 120 wounded. I suspect the low losses were due to Mulligan's impressive breastworks and our soaking the wet hemp bales.

Since exaggerating and lying about casualties was common for both armies, no one knew for sure just where we or our enemies stood. In reality, no one wanted to dwell on the harsh realities of war. All the young men, as young men have down through the ages, thought they were invincible. No one would ever dwell on death very long. It was always there, but death would come to others, not to themselves.

Following the surrender, our prisoners were compelled to hear a speech by our deposed Governor. He scolded them for their invasion of our state and then General Price paroled the chastised Iowans.

I shared a mess tent with several of the Randolph Rangers I had met at Fayette. Two of the boys had suffered minor wounds from cannon shot, but everyone was in high spirits. One of the Rangers boasted, "We just can't be stopped. We licked them at Carthage, we licked em at Oak Hill and we licked 'em here. I hope this teaches them damn Yankees a lesson. I wouldn't be surprised if they just pack up and leave us alone!"

"I wouldn't bet on that happening," another offered.

Lieutenant George Willis was the second in command of the Randolph County Rangers. He had seen me with my militia unit back at Fayette and asked to whom I was assigned. I told him that I had never really officially enlisted with any of the outfits up here since I was still part of the Howard County Militia, most of whom were locked up in the arsenal at St. Louis.

"Well," Willis said while stroking his shaggy beard, "How about joining up with us?" I told him I had been giving it a great deal of thought but I needed to go home and help out on the farm for now. If the war was still going on next year, I told him I would sign up.

"That's the way!" exclaimed the lieutenant, "But I'm sure the hostilities will be over by then. The Yanks will see that we are not to be trifled with and they will tuck tail and leave us alone. Missouri and Kentucky will remain neutral, the Confederacy will prevail and we will eventually leave the old United States of America for our natural place along with the brave fellows of the Confederacy. You mark my words, sir, you mark my words."

Along with Mulligan's army thousands of Springfield muskets and ammunition were captured. A sergeant from the Quartermasters came by in a wagon and dutifully dispensed one of these fine weapons to each of our boys. I declined the offer since I didn't want to lug around another cumbersome ten pound rifle and the shot that goes with it. Besides, I had decided to leave the army and go back home. But for now, I was caught up in the excitement.

General Price assembled the troops, admonishing us to stand by him. He pledged to be faithful to us as well. It was all very moving and I was proud to be a part of it. But it wasn't long before camp life turned monotonous, as it always did, for we young and restless farm boys. The victory celebrations had subsided and the numerous hangovers had come and gone.

The temperature was hot and dry at the end of the month, good traveling weather, so I packed my meager gear, said good-by to my friends and headed back east to Howard County with a thousand stories to tell my family and friends.

As I was leaving, news reached us that the Jayhawker Jim Lane and his Kansas red-legs had lived up to his title of "Grim Chieftain." These "Red-Legs" were known to be even more notorious fiends and robbers than the bastard Jayhawkers. The red leggings they wore had become their distinctive uniform. Lane had finagled a Brigadier commission and was serving as commander of the Army of the western border. His independent Jayhawker expeditions appealed to a large number of low-life thieves and murderers who flocked to join in his exploits. It seems his bunch had been following us at a safe distance as we traveled up to Lexington. Upon reaching the town of Osceola on the banks of the Osage River on September 22nd a drumhead court martial was held. Nine citizens were executed as traitors and the town was burned to the ground. Loading as much of the spoils as they could carry, these upright citizens of the Kansas Territory then high-tailed it for home.

A pro-southern newspaper had recorded a list of the spoils the Jayhawkers' raids had netted. Besides the killing and burning, the party had made off with tons of lead, kegs of powder, barrels of brandy and pounds of sugar, molasses, flour, coffee and bacon. The rich town at the head of navigation on the Osage River for all practical purposes no longer existed. The article also reported that hundreds of horses, mules and cattle were herded to Kansas along with a fine carriage and two pianos which were shipped to Lawrence. It seems that the men helped lighten the load of brandy since most were too drunk to march. It was reported that General Price wanted to pursue the marauders but lacked a sufficient number of men. Many also refused to fight across the Missouri border having signed up to defend their state only.

Chapter Nine

As it was every time I returned home from my various adventures, my family rejoiced and this time Pa literally 'killed the fatted calf.' Ma said she had nearly worn out the pages of her <u>Book of Common Prayer</u> with constant intercessions on my behalf. She alternately laughed and cried and pleaded with me never to do anything like this again.

During and for hours following the family supper I regaled the assembled multitude with vivid descriptions of the battles and the aftermath. I did leave out some of the debauchery experienced by my fellow partisans in taverns and sporting houses. I had stayed clear of those establishments, probably due more to having no money than to an abundance of morals, if I were to be honest. I admit I had partaken of an overabundance of spirits on several occasions, but that was no one's business but my own.

My older brothers listened intently as I relayed my adventures. George William leaned back in his chair and spoke,

"Just think about it. We have actually been at war since 1854. These hostilities have affected all of us. Billy and Jacob. I wish that boy would write and let us know what he was up to. Anyway, y'all have seen a good deal of it first hand. But the Federals out west are just now experiencing what we have been going through. Pa, I've heard you say many a time that this was going to be a short war. And we have had some successes like Oak Hill and Lexington and out east at Manassas, I'll give you that, but this thing is far from over."

Pa said, "George, you show wisdom beyond your years especially for a Howard County dirt farmer." He winked and then continued, "But look at what's going on. Old 'Honest Abe'" (he winked again) "takes over the Federal Government and things go to hell in a hand basket. First South Carolina, well, they have always had more than their fair share of hotheads, and then the rest. Here in Missouri I think that most folks are like me and simply want to be left alone. But, NO! Blair and his puppets keep poking the hornet's nest with a stick. Thank God Billy's call of nature saved him and Jacob. By the way, your fellow patriots were paroled. They had to swear that they wouldn't raise arms against the precious Union. But I'll tell ya, half of the fellows who took the oath headed south to join General Price. After his release, Barker Fristoe stopped by on his way to join the army after the Lexington victory. I said, kind of joshing him, 'Fristoe I was under the impression that you took Mr. Lincoln's oath.' He laughed and said he figured the oath was non-binding since what they done was illegal in the first place. I do believe he was right."

Pa took a deep breath and continued, "Where was I? Oh, yes, Fort Sumter got it started and then there was the Boonville debacle. It wasn't our fault, they caught us with our pants down. Kind of like your experience at Camp Jackson, Billy." He laughed out loud at this, Durette Henry Peyton was in a rare good humor.

"Then we had the opportunity to whip 'em at Carthage and at Wilson Creek and finally at Lexington. I'll give you that the Easterners don't think much about our misery out here. But by God, look what the Yanks got at Manassas Junction.

"Beauregard, Johnson and old Tom Jackson really put it to McDowell's boys. That creek is named Bull Run, but if it were up to me I'd call it 'Yankee Run.'" Pa slapped his knee and laughed at his joke.

Unfortunately for Durette and those who believed that the Yankees would turn tail and sue for peace, events would quickly prove them wrong. Here at home, Union soldiers were turning up all over the place. Steamboats had transported thousands of replacements back to Lexington. Every town along the river was occupied with Germans or Union supporters, the Home Guards. The railroads fed troops to all points of the state, the southwest being the exception. Life in these parts was becoming more and more complicated. Known supporters of states rights and the Missouri State Guard or the Confederacy were under considerable suspicion. Hostile incidents were on the increase. It was becoming more and more common for livestock to be "liberated" by the ever increasing numbers of men in blue. I stayed on the farm and stayed out of sight when we had visitors. After all, I had served the cause and that was enough to get me arrested or forced to take the oath.

And then the news hit our neighborhood like a tornado. On October 28, 1861, in the Masonic Hall in the town of Neosho, Missouri, our duly elected members of the Missouri legislature passed an Act of Secession and joined the Confederacy. It wasn't long before our state, along with Kentucky and the other eleven states, graced the new Confederate battle flag. We came to call it affectionately the 'Stars and Bars.'

Of course this was controversial to those folks who supported the occupation by the federal forces. It is true that this Neosho legislature could not muster a quorum of duly elected officials. So the provisional state government (unelected Union sympathizers forced down our craw) and the U.S. government never accepted the vote to secede as legitimate. But hell, who gave a damn what those invaders thought. They started the thing and by God they forced us to defend our rights.

The local Union men were becoming more and more aggressive towards folks they believed supported the secession, so we were forced to take precautions. As I said, I would hide out, and we built a rugged corral out in the woods that surrounded our place. We hid some horses and mules there along with some wagons filled with corn. Ma also hid her good silver and some of her cherished dishes that had been handed down from our kinfolk back in Virginia.

A couple of days after we became Confederate citizens, at least that's what Pa said, some soldiers came to look over the farm just as Pa had predicted.

Pa welcomed the squad as best he could. Several of the men were sent to take notes. The leader, in broken English, asked to survey the farm and the slave quarters. Aunt Polly was visibly disturbed by their presence while the little girls stared from behind her skirts.

Pa offered the visitors a bottle of his corn liquor which they eagerly accepted. Their leader asked "Gott beer?" Durette chuckled, inspite of the serious nature of their visit, and told then he didn't have beer but he sent them on their way with an ample supply of liquor. Pa laughed after they left.

"Don't worry, boys," he said. "I didn't give them not one drop of the good Williams whiskey. They got the rot gut we make. Funny thing is, though, they didn't know the difference!"

Over time, Fremont's efficiency at controlling southern sympathizers did improve as Federal forces occupied strategic locations. General David Hunter's division occupied Versailles, John Pope secured

Boonville, and Franz Sigel protected the Pacific Railroad terminus at Sedalia. John McKinstry provided Federal security at Tipton and Syracuse. Pro-Union sentiment was strong in this area which was largely populated by German immigrants. We knew all of this because the Union newspapers boldly bragged about the Army's strength.

But we knew it wasn't necessarily true. It was a common belief that one Rebel could whip five Yankees. And I believed that to be the truth!

General Fremont publicly announced his plan to retake Missouri, although he failed to mention the Oak Hill and Lexington engagements, which must have been a cruel embarrassment. One mistake Fremont made was to dismiss the politician Blair since he was 'only' a colonel, apparently overlooking the fact that the Blairs, along with their in-laws the Bentons, were the most powerful Unionists in the state. He had been an outstanding explorer of the far west but he was no politician and Blair resented the fact that Fremont would not offer him the appropriate respect.

Because of this, Fremont's days were numbered. Still, his river operations were successful at preventing southern sympathizers from slipping south to join the victorious Rebel army. His efforts at securing Missouri for the Union had been aided back in July when a pro-Union state government was installed in Jefferson City. Judge Hamilton Gamble was appointed Governor, Willard Hall was appointed

Lieutenant Governor, and Mordecai Oliver became the new Secretary of State.

Since most of the legally elected members of the legislature were in exile, the pro-Union convention that put Gamble and company in office was illegal, but the Federal government was not about to quibble.

The legally elected state officers remained in exile in the southwest part of the state. Missouri now had an official opposition state government which would remain intact until the end of the war.

Every battle fought before our secession on October 28th had been mostly with troops from the Missouri State Guard, a fact of which we were extremely proud. Confederate forces had assisted at Wilson's Creek, but all the battles ultimately had been a state versus the Federal government fight.

It goes without saying that the Confederacy welcomed Missouri into the fold with open arms. The now Confederate state leaders considered their exile to be only a temporary setback and expected to march back to Jefferson City and reclaim their rightfully elected seats in the near future.

Fremont knew he needed to keep Missouri rebel free or he would lose his command. To insure this goal, he led an army back to Springfield, even though this force would be exposed and vulnerable. The Union forces were spared another defeat when in November orders influenced by Blair arrived from Washington City relieving Fremont of his duties and ordering his forces back to the safety of central Missouri for the winter. 1861 would come to an end with neither army victorious over the citizens of the "Show Me" state.

*   *   *

As for me, I had been shown enough. I wanted the war over and I really didn't want any more to do with it. At eighteen, I figured I had experienced enough "adventure" for the rest of my life.

The winter of 1863 seemed to bring things back to normal for my family. Statewide, both sides had hunkered down with minimal activity as they planned for spring campaigns.

The Union Home Guard stationed in Fayette continued their heavy-handed treatment of our pro-Confederate citizens living peacefully in Howard County, but for the most part they left us alone and no major incidents occurred. Yes, it was common for pigs, chickens and a few cattle to disappear mysteriously but the victims of these minor raids generally considered it to be the price they paid for peace from the occupying forces.

Much to my delight, the widow Millicent Yates Park had returned to the Peyton farm and our schooling resumed. My involvement was sporadic since my duties on the farm had increased proportionately for my age. George William and Guffey gave me a hard time for being off 'playing army' while they worked their tails off.

During the day the younger children continued to learn the basics, and on snow days and evenings we devoured the newspapers that Pa procured and lively discussions were quite frequent. Of course the negro Peytons were not privy to these discourses, and it was just as well. It just seemed prudent to avoid getting them all riled up over these debates over the relative merits of their freedom or the lack thereof. Once in a while we would get a letter from Jacob who was now having the time of his life working on a river boat and regaling us with his adventures at Memphis, Vicksburg and even down to the old French town of New Orleans.

Miss Millicent was slowly recovering from her shock and depression over the loss of her gallant husband. I noted that her sorrow seemed now to be evolving into hatred for anyone or anything that had to do with the Union.

The only newspapers available to the family were those printed in St. Louis and an occasional <u>Harper's Weekly</u>. Everything we received was avidly pro-Union and it appeared to us to be highly biased. "Of course, this was to be expected," reflected the always open minded patriarch, "We know they are mostly full of cowflop, and we have to read between the lines, but I'll bet my best mule that the Confederate press is doing the same. You just mark my words!" Pa was never at a loss for an opinion.

East of the Mississippi events were not as dormant as they were in Howard County. In January, the grapevine told of General Jackson's campaign in western Virginia, followed by the news of a Union victory at Mill Springs in Kentucky. In February Union troops captured Fort Henry in Tennessee, which had been seen as a Confederate bulwark against Yankee movement on the Tennessee River. A relatively unknown general by the name of Ulysses Grant was given credit. The fall of Fort Donelson on the 16th of February was a more devastating blow with the surrender of 15,000 Confederates. We also got word that the Union Navy had destroyed the fledgling Confederate Navy off the coast of Elizabeth City, North Carolina.

Even as Confederate forces were victorious in the New Mexico Territory at the battle of Valverde, the partisans' spirits were again dampened by the Union occupation of Nashville. In early March, General John Pope's Union forces headed toward New Madrid, Missouri, while Federal troops clashed with the ill-fated Confederates at the battle of Elk Horn Tavern at Pea Ridge, Arkansas. News of this Confederate loss lay like a pall over our friends and neighbors.

Our Missouri boys had proudly marched again under the leadership of General Price, fondly called "Old Pap." General McCulloch's division had been there along with several others. Our state guard numbered about 5,500 of the entire force of 8,000. General Van Dorn was the overall commander.

Confederate losses hovered around 1,400 men. Survivors lamenting over the losses of battle swore that it was General Van Dorn's failure and the deaths of two fighting generals, McCulloch and McIntosh, that brought it about. It was strongly held that if either of these two generals had lived the outcome of the battle would have been entirely different.

The pain of loss reached home with the death of a prominent Boone County native, Private Bruce Bell. I learned later that a letter professing his love and the locket he wore with the image of his wife were carried back to her. Upon hearing the news, Miss Millicent wept at the losses all young women and parents shared. She said that a bitter gall rose once more in her throat and that she had not known that she was capable of hating the Yankees more, but that she did.

The Confederate loss at Pea Ridge kept the Union's fragile control of our state in place, at least for the present, while in St. Louis the newspapers touted the belief that peace was at hand.

But peace did not reign supreme yet. A vicious cycle was developing. The increased hostility of the occupiers precipitated a growth of partisan bands whose presence brought about an increase in Union forces; and on and on it continued. Experienced men branded as "Bushwhackers" were making their presence felt. I'm sure I had served with many of these fellows, and much to my surprise I felt a twinge of pride for doing so. Battles to the east could rage on, but out here it was still what the newspapers called a battle between "Jayhawks" and "Border Ruffians." That battle had already been raging for years.

Following Pea Ridge, General Price's Army struggled through the cold winter of 1862. Food and clothing were scarce and many of our loyal Missourians, like me, I guess, chose to go home for the winter. Some of our boys decided that they could serve the cause better as bushwhackers, cutting telegraph lines, burning bridges, ambushing Union patrols and generally raising hell among the Union Army and its' supporters.

On December 22, 1861, the new Commander of the Union Department of Missouri had issued something called General Order Number 31. General Henry Halleck's order proclaimed that anyone caught destroying government property would be shot, and essentially everything was government property due to the imposition of martial law. This did not matter, as paroled prisoners ignored the loyalty oath, considering it to be illegal anyway, as significant numbers of the State Guard preferred to fight the war from the comfort of their own hearths. General Order 31 ignited the spark that only escalated the bloody guerrilla war in Missouri.

The prevailing opinion from the out of state occupiers was that every Missourian was a secessionist. Since all were considered rebels, payment from the local treasurers and shop keepers was extracted to pay for damages done to the Union infrastructure.

The Kansas Jayhawkers continued their raids on the Missouri side of the border. In order to stem the violence and stamp out the "secesh" once and for all, Halleck issued an even harsher order. On March 13, 1862, General Order Number 2 sent shock waves throughout the state. This order explained that Confederate guerrillas were not soldiers but outlaws, and they would be summarily shot.

Pa snorted, "Well, if it's good for the goose, it's good for the gander. Old Henry Halleck has done it now. Our boys will give as good or better as they get. Ain't no Yankee safe now. Hard times are getting harder!"

Things got worse in July when General Order No. 19 came down the pike. This missive ordered all able-bodied Missouri men of fighting age to join the Union Militia. This forced young men to choose sides, often reluctantly. Over 52,000 joined the militia but a significant number declined and slipped south to join the Confederacy or took to the road as partisan fighters.

A noted example was Frank James. James had been in General Price's army but was left behind due to sickness. He was captured and paroled after taking the "oath." Recovered and happy back on the farm in Clay County, near Kearney, Order 19 sent him into the bush, soon to be followed by his younger brother Jesse. Order number 19 did help the Union in ferreting out some authentic rebels. Unfortunately the order also allowed for the settling of old scores and injustice often prevailed.

Though initially against guerilla warfare, President Jefferson Davis was forced to come to terms with this phenomena. He came to realize that there were large numbers of Confederate supporters living in occupied states like Missouri, and that irregular warfare diverted Union troops and disrupted their war efforts. On April 21, 1862, the Confederate Congress passed the Partisan Ranger Act commissioning partisans for independent duty.

I was now faced with Order 19.

"There is no way in hell I will join the damned Dutch militia," I said over supper one hot August evening. "I fought for the cause at Oak Hill and Lexington and I did my duty. But damn it all, I just don't have the *war fever* that is going around. Pa, this just ain't my war."

My father thought for a moment and then, looking me square in the eye, he responded, "Well, Billy, that man Halleck has made it your war. I'm too old, so I don't have to choose, but son, I understand the dilemma you are in. You have served your state with honor already. You're not a violent man, but that sonofabitch Halleck is going to make you one!"

Pa was right, I had to admit. Not to decide is to decide. So I told Pa that I thought it was time for me to head across the river and join the boys down at Neosho. George William said he had no love for the Yankees, but he was going to join the Federal militia over at Fayette so he could at least be closer to home. I was speechless. It looked as if George was going to be what we called "Paw Paws,' southern sympathizers, serving the Union because of Order number 19.

"What about you?" I asked Guffey. He said he reckoned he'd go with me. "Well, I'll be damned," I spouted. Pa didn't say a word and Ma broke into tears as she ran from the room.

Chapter Ten

Out east the war had been raging hot and heavy. We lost the fight back at Shiloh Church in April and the Mississippi River was chock full of Union Iron-clads. We have had no word from Jacob for several months and we are all very concerned about his welfare especially since New Orleans also fell back in April.

I couldn't help but wonder about what was going on down there. We heard that the good ladies of that town didn't take too kindly to the Yankee overlords and had taken to demonstrating their contempt by spitting or dumping their chamber pots on the unsuspecting blue coated victims. These acts prompted the head Federal Commander, General Benjamin Butler, to issue his infamous General Order Number 28, which directed that any woman who showed contempt toward the boys in blue "be treated as a woman of the town plying her avocation." Some general orders work better than others since we are told that insults decreased immediately.

Most of the fall harvest was completed, and Guffey and I were getting tired of hiding out from the ever increasing Federal patrols. George William had taken the oath and was hauled off to Sedalia for sentry duty. So much for being near home.

On the same day, September 24th, that the Union President suspended the writ of Habeas Corpus for anyone who helps a secessionist, Guffey and I saddled up our horses with all the necessities for a long trip and slipped away in the early morning fog.

Guffey was mounted on Pepper, his prized gelding. Pa had insisted that my horse Calico was not a fit mount for a Missouri cavalryman so he gave me a beautiful black stallion, named, you guessed it, Blackey. Federal troops regularly patrolled the main roads and we knew if spotted we would be arrested as partisan supporters. I was armed with my Navy colt which increased that risk. On the other hand, we were aided by a different, but equally effective "underground railroad" that existed for those who wished to join General Price's army.

Southern sympathizers would hide the travelers during the day. Union scouting parties would seldom venture out after dark, so it was relatively easy to move in the evening. Near Lexington we knew of a friendly ferry operator who would clandestinely move riders and horses across the big river in the late hours of the night. Many made use of it even though travel like this was dangerous for both those who hid and those who did the hiding. Order Number 2 was not a vague threat but an active reality. We knew of several cases where innocent hunters were executed simply because they were carrying guns.

Guffey and I essentially retraced the border route south of Harrisonville that Jacob and I had followed back in 1858. It was area where the Unionists wouldn't venture, so we could then travel safely and openly. It was not long before we met up with other young men who were reacting in the same way to the general order.

Meanwhile, back in Howard County, the provost marshals were tightening the noose on known slave holders. In spite of Fremont's emancipation proclamation being rescinded by Lincoln there were still hotheads in the local governments and militias who continued to implement his vision.

It was a mild November morning when Mrs. Millicent Yates Park harnessed her buggy, kissed her parents good-by and headed south to resume her teaching duties. The trip went smoothly at first. She stopped at a friend's house for lunch and conversation. Back on the road, Milly marveled at how her life had changed. She pondered the strength she had gained from the support given her by the Yates and the Peytons. She was looking forward to assuming her teaching role and to the lively discussions around the Peyton dinner table. But there was no place in her heart, mind or soul for forgiveness regarding the Yankee occupation force. At times, she would almost forget the pain of the loss of her young husband and then the all too common sight of a blue uniform would bring it all back.

As the buggy rounded a bend in the road, Milly was again forced to confront the source of her misery. Three uniformed soldiers stood in the middle of the road signaling for her to stop. Her throat tightened and her heart raced at the sight of the enemy now so close. As the buggy drew up next to the men, the leader of the small squad spoke in broken English.

"Vat is your name?" Before she could answer he continued, "Ver are you going? Get out! Now!" Millicent stepped out of the buggy and pulled her shawl tightly around her shoulders. In spite of the mildness of the afternoon, she suddenly experienced a chill running from the nape of her neck to the tip of her toes.

The leader, a sergeant she thought, barked an order to the others in German. They immediately removed the trunks and packages from the buggy and started rummaging through them, throwing her clothing on the ground. As a box of books was dumped her shock turned to anger.

"Stop it," she shouted, "Who do you think you are?" The men continued their work, laughing menacingly. Millicent suddenly realized that the soldiers were drunk. Her anger turned to stone cold fear. The leader turned toward her and slapped her across the face, hard. "Shut up!" he shouted.

Tears welled in her eyes as the pain of the blow spread. But then, instead of meekly submitting to the German's abuse, she hit him back with all the power she could muster. The hate she had been harboring for months exploded.

"Got damm you, you whore!" the sergeant yelled.

Millicent was punched again and again. Her petticoats were torn from her body. One of the other soldiers grabbed her hair and pulled her head backwards. A sharp pain to her stomach was her last clear memory.

The ordeal did not last long, but Millicent felt as if the rape had lasted a lifetime. The sergeant threw her to the ground and had his way with her. When he finished, another took his place. Fortunately, the third man declined to engage in the assault. Just a teenager, his companions derided him but he turned and ran to the horses.

Everything was a blur to Millicent. As if in slow motion the Germans mounted their horses and rode off leaving her in the dirt. Her body ached everywhere. She felt like her body had been totally violated. She rose to her feet, staggered toward her buggy, and vomited. Eventually, she was able to continue her journey and reached the Peyton place before dark.

Guffey and I had joined up with some of the boys from Randolph County and several others from Howard County who had been paroled in St. Louis. About mid-morning on the first day of December, a cold but dry day, Jack Jefferson returned from a furlough back in Higbee, a little crossroads community about five miles from our place.

"Billy, can I talk to you for a minute?" he asked. His stark expression sent a chill through me and my companions. Everyone knew that Jack could not be bringing good news. We walked over toward a grove of black jack oak. "What's going on," I asked. "Are Ma and Pa alright?"

"Yes, Billy, everyone is alright I guess," Jack explained. "It's just that the god damned Dutch done messed with Miss Millicent." As Jack relayed the story as best he could, my blood began to boil. A quiet rage descended on me that I had never before experienced.

When Jack had said all he could say about the incident I grabbed my friend by the shoulder saying, "Tell no one about this. Let's say that one of my favorite mares was stolen by the Dutch. Yes, that's it. One of my mares is gone. That's enough information to quiet these boys curiosity," I said, nodding over my shoulder towards my fellow rebels. "Tell no one, Jack," I continued. "It ain't nobody's business."

"You're right, Billy. When your Pa told me this he swore me to secrecy. Nobody knows except your kin and the niggers. Everybody loves Miss Milly and nobody going to hurt her no more, she's already gone through enough hell. We don't need to be adding to her misery." Jack kicked the dirt as he spoke. I told him that even Guffey was not to know of this terrible event that had taken place on a dirty road in Howard County. I sensed something that felt like flint striking steel flash across my eyes. I knew that Jack had seen it too.

Later that evening I went to visit our captain. Captain Evans was only a few years older than me and we had essentially grown up together. I slapped him a salute saying, "Sir, I request permission to speak freely."

"Certainly," he replied, "and cut the horse shit, Billy. What's on your mind?"

I elaborated on the lie about the mare being stolen, adding that Pa was sick and I would like to go home for a spell and see if I could make things right. Everyone understood that there would be no campaigning during the winter months and provisions were getting scarce. It wasn't uncommon to grant such requests so I was given a letter explaining 'to whom it may concern' that I was a member of the Missouri Faction of the Confederate Army and had been granted a leave of absence.

The next morning, loaded down with a saddle bag filled with hard tack biscuits and letters from my brother and others from the Howard County Company, I struck off for home.

Things were a bit trickier as I neared Cole Camp. The partisans who gave me shelter also advised me of scouting movements and safer trails. My anger was still white hot and growing with every mile closer to Howard County.

Early one evening, since I was now traveling at night, I stumbled upon a group of Home Guard coming over a rise in the road. I found myself smack dab

in the middle of a five man scout group. The moon
was not yet light enough to allow me to see their fea-
tures clearly but I could see enough. Neither side
had been aware of the other since the sound of our
horses hooves had covered each others noise. For a
moment I froze in the saddle. I knew that I would be
searched and probably shot on the spot. Instinctively, I made a friendly gesture as I yelled, "Thank
God I found you. There are some rebel bushwhackers about a mile down the road." As the squad
members squinted to see past me, I raised a newly
acquired Springfield to my shoulder and fired point
blank into the lead man. Flame and smoke billowed
from the muzzle as my surprised horse reared. Two
of the patrols' mounts turned and galloped back
down the road throwing their unsuspecting riders.
The fellow I shot held on to the reins with one hand
and grasped the right side of his chest with the
other. In a flash I saw that the Federal was no older
than me.

I spurred Blackey and we galloped ahead. Another man who had regained his composure came
charging at me at full speed. For a brief second, I
remembered reading about scenes like these with
knights in jousting contests. But this was not a ficti-
tious tale of yesteryear, it was a life or death struggle
happening in the here and now. I grabbed my empty
rifle by the barrel and hit the man with the stock in a
movement similar to the countless swings I had
made with a scythe during the wheat harvest.

The blow landed squarely across my opponent's body. I had hit him so hard that the rifle split in two and it felt like my arms were on fire. With a yell that conveyed both hate and fear, I struck off after the remaining mounted Yankee. He was still in the saddle untouched by my wrath, frozen in time staring at what remained of his companions. I simply passed him by.

I caught up with two of the frantic riderless horses who had now settled down a bit. I gathered their reins and quietly slipped into the woods. My heart was pounding so hard I feared the Federals would hear it.

I had dismounted and was carefully picking my way through the darkness leading the horses and trying not to break a leg or make any undue noise. I didn't have to worry, I guess, since no one was chasing me, but I knew it wouldn't be long before the alarm was raised. I knew I had perpetrated serious damage upon at least two of the soldiers and that the militia would be on full alert. My throat was dry and as I took a swig from my canteen I discovered much to my surprise that I was shaking. Reaching into my saddle bag I retrieved a pint of brandy Guffey had given me and I pulled a swig. This brought about a coughing fit, but it didn't matter. The burning liquid was bringing me back to the reality of what had just occurred.

I took another drink and started to settle down. Had I killed those two boys? I had been around kill-

ing for some time now but it had never been me doing the killing. I had never thought I would have to.
I had been in two battles and never fired a shot, and
I naively thought, I guess, that I could help without
shooting someone. How very wrong I was!

But I had, in fact, been in real danger. I still was,
since it had been less than an hour since I had encountered my enemy. I had been careless. In a
hurry to get home I had ignored the warnings and
had ridden straight into the scouting patrol. Now the
whole countryside would be up in arms. This was
occupied territory with many Union supporters living
here. Why had I been so stupid? And what about
those Yankees I had scattered all over the Cole Camp
Road? How many were hurt?

"Settle down, Billy," I muttered out loud, "Settle
down." Slowly I formulated a plan of action. First I
surveyed the treasures I had captured. Both of the
Home Guard horses carried saddle bags, canteens of
water, fresh biscuits and some delicious smelling
ham. There were also several pint bottles of home
brew. The shaking in my hands was still there, and
for a moment I considered calming my nerves with
the Yankee whiskey, but wiser thoughts prevailed. I
forced myself to think. I had to act, and act fast.
Besides the food and drink, one of the saddle bags
contained two Navy Colt .36 caliber revolvers
wrapped in oil cloth. They looked as if they had
never been fired and for a moment I forgot the predicament I was in. These guns had pearl handles

and the brass hardware shone like gold in the moon-
light. I must have died and gone to heaven, I
thought. I now possessed three Colts that rivaled
those of Colonel Townsend. And then the reality hit
me that I might actually get to heaven sooner than I
liked if I didn't get my ass in gear. Breathe, Billy,
breathe, I told myself.

The adrenalin rush was subsiding and the shakes
had finally gone. Loading everything I could on
Blackey, I removed the saddles and bridles of the
captured mounts and set them free. I would have
loved to have kept them, but they would have
slowed me down.

I loaded all the pistols and carefully stuck them
in my belt. All of a sudden I felt famished. I devoured some of the biscuits and ham. I passed up
the whiskey but indulged in another sip of my
brandy. I then carefully picked my way through to a
trail I found and headed northwest to the friendlier
town of Clinton.

At daybreak I unpacked my gear and hobbled
Blackey so he could graze in a lush pasture nearby.
I leaned against a tree with the Colts within reach
and slept the sleep of the dead. I knew that there
must be folks looking for me but I was too tired to
care. If they found me we would just have to fight it
out. Fortunately, no one came by my hiding place
and I was able to sleep safely. It must have been
about noon when I awoke with a start. It took a
moment for me to remember where I was and that I

was on the run.

I ate again, and as I gnawed on my biscuits and ham I pondered the events of last evening. Many amazing things had happened but I was starting to appreciate how things had turned out. Yes, I had let my guard down but I had survived and had caused damage to the occupying Union war machine. How much, I didn't know, but certainly to their pride if nothing else.

The village of Cole Camp was alive with activity. Known southern sympathizers had been driven out of the area and their property burned or confiscated. It was not a rebel friendly community. I couldn't help but laugh out loud when I heard stories of what was being said at Cole Camp about my impromptu raid.

Five men in their own Home Guard had been assaulted by a bushwhacker raiding party. It was not known how many rebels there were but it was rumored that there had been a dozen or more considering the damage they had done. One of the boys had been shot and knocked from his horse, but the bullet had hit a Bible he carried in his left pocket and folks said the word of God had saved him. Two other riders had been thrown but nothing serious had happened to them. The most seriously wounded soldier had been knocked from his horse when one of the raiders had smacked him with a rifle butt. Thankfully for him, the blow missed his head which would certainly have been fatal. The blow hit his shoulder blade and arm and folks say it will take months for his injuries to heal. All but one had suffered miscellaneous sprains, cuts and bruises.

Down at the general store the gossip was that a whole company of Confederates had swooped down on the unsuspecting Home Guard, done their mischief, and then disappeared into thin air. Like ghosts, it was said. All roads leading to Sedalia and points north were to be heavily patrolled.

To the south, a company of Germans from St. Louis were scouting the area but reported that the rebels must have slipped the noose and gone back to Springfield. The Home Guard survivors of their severely trying experience had very little to say regarding their ordeal.

I was well rested and alert so I continued my journey. The next evening I slept in the hayloft of a partisan family at their farm near Clinton. By weeks end news of a rebel raid bravely thwarted by the Cole Camp Home Guard had made the St. Louis papers.

Slowly and carefully, having learned my lesson, I made my way home. Travel, even among like-minded supporters, was dangerous for a young man without the proper papers, but folks took care of me along the way. It was getting colder but at least it remained dry.

I finally made it safely home without any further dustups. My family was delighted to have me back safe and sound, but Pa warned everyone that discretion was the order of the day. Everyone, white and colored, pledged their secrecy. The local magistrate from Fayette had been by inquiring after the missing Peyton boys and the family was under more scrutiny than usual.

Miss Millicent had recovered, at least physically, from her ordeal and valiantly tried to be sociable. Not a word was openly spoken by anyone regarding the rape, but Pa had whispered to me that Milly, fortunately, was not pregnant and had also escaped the all too prevalent soldiers' venereal diseases.

Pa's spies had quietly investigated the local German units and it had not taken long to discover who the bastards were. Over large quantities of beer the rapists had publicly teased their companion who had not joined them in their fun. Their names and the location of their living quarters were passed on to Pa, who upon discovering the reason for my early return, shared this information with me.

"What are we going to do?" Pa asked one evening after the family had gone to bed. I quietly answered,

"The most important thing for me is that no one know I'm back. That way no one can link what I'm going to do with us or the Yates. And Pa," I said with unexpected hatred in my voice, "the less you know the better."

For several days and evenings I shadowed my targets. I pondered the events that had changed the naïve gentle boy that I had been into the steely eyed stalker I had become. And then, just before Christmas, my chance at revenge became a reality.

I had been masquerading as a crippled old man. The ragged clothing and an affected limp allowed me to move among the citizens virtually unnoticed.

I had been tailing the leader of the Dutch rapists all evening. It was easy since the men were anticipating the birth of Our Lord with large flagons of beer most evenings. I was huddled under a ragged blanket in an empty doorway across from the tavern they were occupying. And then, much to my delight, the object of my hatred stumbled out the door all alone. He headed back down the alley passing directly in front of me. I stood and followed him when suddenly he stopped and unbuttoned his trousers and started to relieve himself on the side of the building.

"God damned Dutch," I muttered as my blood started to boil. I had never known that the hate that welled up in me regarding this low life man could even exist. As I approached him the German turned and slurred,

"Vat da hell you be looking at?"

Those were his last words on this earth. The ten inch blade of my Bowie knife was violently inserted through his back directly into his heart. I was furious but almost laughed as he stood for a moment with a blank stare, holding his prick as he continued to piss. Then it was over. He crumpled into his own mess as I walked away. No one had seen my wrath. One down. As I carefully walked home I briefly regretted that my plan didn't allow for a long pro-

tracted torture session, but at least I got the job
done.

Slipping through the darkness I consoled myself
with the knowledge that two more of the bastards
remained. It might be a bit more risky now since the
killing could alert the others. Maybe not. Fayette
had become a violent place and murder was not uncommon. And besides, my plan was worth the risk.
It felt strangely cleansing to have avenged Miss Milly
in this way, and what the hell, I wanted the other
two sonsabitches to know fear.

Fortunately, I was right about the military not
raising an alarm. The Provost Marshall was not
greatly concerned regarding the incident, as drunken
brawls and killings were common among the lower
ranks. He did launch a perfunctory investigation
and went on his daily business of harassing my fellow secessionists. None of the officials seemed to
worry about that sergeant's death. But Sergeant
Heinrick and Corporal Vogel knew differently. Unnoticed by the morticians, the two friends who went to
view the body immediately saw the piece of bloody
petticoat lodged in the dead man's breast pocket. I
had asked Aunt Polly to cut me a piece of this dread-
ful reminder.

For the next week, Sergeant Heinrich cautiously
checked his surroundings for anything or anyone
suspicious. He must have wished he could tell the
authorities that the murder of that stupid leader was
a revenge killing perpetrated by friends or family of

the woman they had raped. But of course this was out of the question, since knowledge by his superiors would bring about their immediate execution. So, he did the best he could, I guess, being vigilant and keeping away from lonely isolated locations.

It was now Christmas eve. Heinrich's unit had been dismissed from their regular duties and had ridden down river to a friendly German settlement outside of Rocheport. The local Union supporting citizens had organized an extravaganza. The morning after was spent sobering up and preparing for the trip back to camp at Fayette. Heinrich and Vogel had enjoyed the local hospitality to the fullest and were experiencing the after effects of the party as they slowly rode west towards their quarters. The road was empty except for occasional bands of soldiers plodding slowly along. I had been hiding in a draw near the road. When the two men I had been stalking rode by I slipped into the road behind them. As I pulled up next to them in my "borrowed" Yankee uniform they greeted me in their native tongue.

"I don't speak Dutch," I said. It seems as if the one they called Heinrich had experienced far too many mornings such as this since he turned to me and in English wondered why he continued to drink so much when he was well aware of the next day's consequences.

Turning to his partner he asked, "Why do we do this to our bodies? My head is splitting and I feel like throwing up again. Will I ever learn? The chaplain says that the morning after miseries are the wages of sin. What does he know about sin? Perhaps he is right. What do you think, English? You must not have had as much beer as we did last night." We three horsemen were now passing through a heavily wooded area. Up ahead was a small creek and low water ford. "What's the matter with you, friend, are you more hung over than I am?" Heinrich continued.

Suddenly I sat up straight in the saddle, pulled my horse to a stop and said, "Go to hell, you sonofabitch!" From under my coat two Navy Colts were pointing directly at the pair. Before either man could respond, I fired the revolvers at point blank range. The first shot hit Heinrich in the stomach. The second hit the one called Vogel in the throat knocking him from his horse. Heinrich slumped forward in the saddle as his horse reared and then floundered down the creek bed throwing the stunned rider into the shallow water. The depression at the creek bed and the surrounding thicket had deadened the sound and hid the deadly scene from sight, just as I had planned. Without even looking back I slowly rode up the rise waving at the men ahead who had stopped to inquire about the sound of gunfire. Assuming that the men were still celebrating, they turned and continued on their journey. I slipped off on a side trail and quickly rode north away from the grisly scene. By the time the bodies were discovered and a scouting party organized I was safely back at the Peyton farm, having destroyed the Union uniform that Pa's contact had procured.

In my own very personal way, I was having a splendid Christmas. I had heard of some friendly partisan bands who had been disrupting Union activities out west in Platt County. The next evening, without fanfare, I rode away. It was clear to me now where fate had led me. The months of indecision faded into history as I looked forward to a life of bushwhacking. The raw emotions that had been festering in my heart had erupted into a full fledged case of unadulterated disgust. The animosity I held was now a white hot personal hatred of any supporter of the Union.

Any friend of Abraham Lincoln would never be a friend of mine!

Chapter Eleven

For years the irregular war along the Kansas-Missouri border had been honing the skills of partisans on both sides of the slavery issue. My exposure to the violence of the war was only a small incident in the spiraling reprisals that continued to plague the area.

William Quantrill, a former school teacher, had made a name for himself in the border wars and was actively recruiting in and around Kansas City.

A letter finally arrived from my cousin Jacob Walker who said he had been initially influenced by the militia, but still chose to follow his dream as a river pilot. The Peyton household was buzzing in excitement with his news. He told how he had served in a Hannibal, Missouri Militia Unit with a young man who was a licensed Mississippi river pilot. This young man had introduced him to the ways of the river. Then the Yankees had marched in, and the militia had disbanded. The men had gone their separate ways, most heading down river to meet up with Confederate troops under the command of ex-Mayor of St. Joseph, Jeff Thompson. Thompson now car-

ried the romantic nickname "Swamp Fox" and held a
brigadier's commission in the Confederate military
district of southeast Missouri.

Jacob's friend Sam had decided to abandon the
turmoil of the nation's hostilities and had headed to
Carson City, Nevada with his brother. Before he left,
Sam had given Jacob the names of some connections
in the steamboat industry in Memphis. Jacob
hitched a ride down river with some friends and
eventually ended up working on a Confederate gunboat up on the head waters of the Yazoo River in
Mississippi. I assumed all was well and good with
Jacob, at least as good as things could be in the circumstances.

*   *   *

After arriving up in Platte County I asked a few
discreet questions and finally was introduced to one
of Quantrill's captains by the name of William Anderson. Anderson was not much older than me and it
was rumored that he had a very mean streak. He
seemed normal enough to me, but who knows. Besides, I was developing a bit of a mean streak myself.

Meanwhile, back in Howard County, ominous
clouds of an escalating conflict were scudding across
the landscape. A detachment from the 19th Iowa
volunteer infantry was stationed in Fayette since
there were not enough Union supporters in the
county to constitute a Federal Home Guard. This

area was the heart of our discontent and the few Union supporters who had lived there before the war had either hightailed it out of there or had laid low. There were some exceptions, however. A few grabbed the reins of the power void and ran with them.

One day as the Peytons were finishing breakfast the dogs started barking an alarm long before the clatter of hooves could be heard down the lane.

According to our hired hand, Junior Smith, this is how the events of the day unfolded. Junior had struck off to find me as soon as the blue coated bastards had left. It seems as if my Pa had stepped from the house to speak with the dozen or so blue clad visitors. Pa started to welcome the men but the captain of the guard spoke first.

"Mr. Peyton, I would be much obliged if you would muster the members of your family and your niggers also."

Pa replied, I don't own any slaves, sir. These coloreds are part of the widow Walker's estate." He then turned to one of the younger children and told him to do as the soldier had said. After all had gathered in the front yard the captain pulled a paper from inside his jacket.

"Mr. Peyton, I want you to listen very closely to what I'm going to read and then you can explain what it means to your niggers."

Durette stood tall and firm as he said, "Sir, everyone in this party is savvy enough to understand anything you have to say, so proceed."

The captain huffed, but unfolded the paper and read: "This is an order issued back on August 30th, 1861, by Major General Fremont. You must have heard about it?"

"Yes," Durette offered, "I've heard about it. It is my understanding that the President has rescinded that order."

"Oh but you are wrong. Let me refresh your memory. This order," the captain shouted while waving the document in the air, "put your fair state under martial law. And I also hope you remember that this means that men bearing arms without proper authority, like I'm told two of your sons do, will be court-martialed and shot." The captain nodded to his sergeant who, with his men, dismounted and started searching the outbuildings and then the main house. The captain continued his pompous lecture,

"You may also recall that Major General Fremont ordered that slaves belonging to anyone disloyal to the United States were to be freed. Do you remember that?"

"As I said before, I do not own any slaves and more importantly I am a loyal citizen of the United States. To the best of my knowledge, Missouri is still in the Union. Of course there was that business down at Neosho, but I guess that remains to be seen."

Junior was speaking faster and had started to stutter.

"Slow down, dammit," I said.

He continued, "A man by the name of Wyllis Curtis and wearing mostly civilian clothing, except for a military forage cap, spurred his horse forward. Your Pa knew him as a poor dirt farmer and merchant who owned a small hardware store in Franklin and who for years had been an avid abolitionist.

"How dare you, you sonofabitch," he said through clenched teeth, "you have not heard the last of this."

Slowly he rode to the cluster of Negroes and said,

"Do you understand that you can be free? You no longer have to suffer under the yoke of oppression."

Rufus, the oldest of Aunt Polly's sons, stepped forward and said, "We aints oppressed, sir. We got it good."

Curtis wheeled his horse and joined the ranks of the soldiers who were now mounted after their unsuccessful search. Without a word, the squad turned and headed back down the lane.

I later learned what happened next down at the Negro quarters. That evening, Rufus and his brothers were discussing the morning's events.

"You know it's not true. Old man Lincoln don't want to free no slaves," Obadiah, the younger brother said.

Jebodiah said, "We really don't need Mr. Lincoln. We can leave anytime we want. They got this railroad that will help us get to Iowa, or Canada, or even to New York. Then we can do anything we want."

"What do you mean?" Rufus interjected. "What

are you going to do? Farm? That's all any of us knows how to do. What's so different about farming in Canada than here? We don't got no money to buy our own place, so we winds up working for somebody else. Somebody who ain't family like Miz Walker and the Peytons. Just what you think that would be like? You is a fool!"

Jebodiah spit back, "No, I'm not! You is da fool. Can't you see the handwritin' on the wall? Them Yankees have already won. It's just a matter of time. Sho nuff, it's true, them people have cared for us all our lives and they is good folks. But they is the exception. Look how them other niggers is treated. Families split up. Some sold to Mexico to work in the mines. Others got to work the cane fields down south. Shit! That ain't no way to live. Sometimes I think they made a big mistake by teaching us to read and write. I'm leaving and there ain't nothing any of you can say to keep me from it. And that's that!" I was told he stormed out after that and hasn't been seen by anyone here since.

*   *   *

I'd been looking for Bill Anderson, and I'd found him, seated alone at a table in the saloon of the Main Hotel in Platte City. Several seriously tough looking young men lounged near the door. Sure I had heard stories of some of these fellows exploits and I figured that we might share a few things in common. I did recognize several of the guerillas I had seen before. There was the notorious Fletch Taylor along with James Little and Joe Hart. A boy not much younger than me was slouched at another table with several other well armed members of Quantrill's partisan rangers.

As I approached Anderson, one of the men from the other table rose and held out a raised hand.

"Just a moment, pilgrim," he said, "state your business."

I stopped in my tracks and said, "Excuse me, sir, I wish to have a conversation with Mr. Anderson."

"Well," the bearded partisan drawled, "You may wish to speak with him, but he may not wish to speak with you."

I asked, "And who might you be, sir?"

"I'm just a Platte County farmer, but I reckon you can call me Mr. James, Mr. Frank James."

Looking him in the eye I said, "Well, Mr. James, it's this way. My name is Billy Peyton and I'm on the run from the Federals. I'd like to join your company.

"Alright, Mr. Billy Peyton, I think it's time you spoke with 'Bloody' Bill."

William Anderson was a handsome man, not quite six feet tall, with long curly hair and a short beard and mustache. At first glance he might have passed as a mild mannered shopkeeper or teacher, but a second look would reveal the danger in his eyes. He was dressed in what was commonly known as a bushwhacker costume.

Most of the men wore loose fitting large pocketed hunting shirts with fancy embroidery across the front. Anderson was dressed entirely in black. Some woman, a sister or sweetheart I supposed, had sewn ornate garlands on the bib and sleeves. He wore a cocked hat with a variety of ribbons and a star shaped pin attached to a large plume.

His trousers were tucked into knee-high boots with silver spurs adorning the heels. This outfit might bring about a few chuckles back home, were it not for what it symbolized. The most important accessory to this bushwhacker's attire was the belt and holsters containing two Navy Colt pistols. I felt strangely akin to this man as I felt my own purloined pistols securely fastened to my side.

The object of my scrutiny had been born and raised in Randolph County, Missouri, just a few miles north of our farm, but had moved with his family to the Kansas Territory before the war. In early 1863, his sisters along with some other pro-southern women were arrested and imprisoned in a rickety building at 14th Street and Grand Avenue in Kansas City. The wind and rain were more than the structure could stand and early one August morning the building collapsed, killing his eldest sister Josephine, sixteen, and severely injuring the others. Mary Ellen was crippled for life and the youngest, Janie, just ten years old, suffered lacerations, broken legs and an injured back. Three other women prisoners were also killed. On the day this tragic news reached Anderson terror was launched on anyone wearing Federal blue.

Quantrill, the Younger brothers and other bush-whackers were often known to show compassion and spare some of their captives. But not so with Ander-son. As with all of the famous partisans, Anderson was a crack shot with his Navy revolvers and an ac-complished horseman. It was said he could swing from the saddle at a full gallop and pluck a pistol from the ground. Anderson was immensely popular among his followers. He was a rigorous disciplinar-ian but extremely fair. He was known to be without fear in battle and recorded the number of his victims by tying knots on a silk cord. The 53 knots he had tied by the end of his life were surpassed only by his compatriot Archie Clemmens who had 54.

It didn't take long for some boys who had just ar-rived here from home to fill me in on what was going on back at the homestead. Aunt Sophie was beside herself and the rest of her family was hysterical. I guess Jebodiah had taken it upon himself to follow his dream and had headed out to "greener pastures." But on his way he had done something terrible to all of us. It wasn't so much that Jeb had left, because they had suspected that that was what he planned to do for some time. They, and everyone else, were hor-rified because he had been talking to the Federals. The Yankees had promised to help him go to New York or someplace else if he would spill the beans about what was going on in our family. And he did.

He told them how and where we hid our livestock and most damning of all, that I had murdered the three soldiers that had raped Miss Millicent.

This news brought the complacent Peyton clan to life. Pa buried everything of value, some coins and silver plate, along with the family bible and important papers. Everyone gathered up what they could. Wagons were filled with stores from the smokehouse and root cellar. With the most valued furniture piled high on the wagons, everyone but Pa and the Negroes left for the relative safety of family over at Rocheport.

There wasn't anything for Pa to do but wait, and he didn't have to wait long. They came the next morning. They were the same Federals that had visited the homestead before. My Pa met the Captain of the guard at the front gate.

Before he could speak, the Captain signaled the troopers to dismount. The gist of the matter was later detailed in a letter Ma sent to me from Rocheport.

It was a heart breaking document. Ma said that the Federals had arrested Pa for treason. They said that he had been giving aid and comfort to the enemy at the peril of his family and property. Pa told Ma he reckoned this was all true but that he had informed the Federals that it was all bullshit!

The bastards had lit torches and were fixing to set fire to the place when Pa grabbed the Captain and pulled him off his horse. Pa said that in retrospect this was a stupid thing for him to do since all it accomplished was a bump on the head from a Springfield rifle. The house was torched and Pa was thrown on a wagon as they headed toward the Glasgow Road.

I don't know what other damage they did or how our negroes fared. All I knew was that the guards said they were going to make an example out of Pa.

I was enraged. I stomped over to Frank James and relayed the contents of the letter to him. I was on the verge of tears. Frank listened quietly until I finished my diatribe. There was fire in his eyes as he said that these actions could not go unpunished. Pa had lost everything the family had worked for and was waiting to be hung in Glasgow, Missouri.

*   *   *

At the start of 1863 the war was still raging with no end in sight. Out east the Confederate forces were holding their own as both armies continued to trade bloody blows. The President of the United States had caused quite a stir throughout the country with his Emancipation Proclamation. This document was introduced to us on the first of January and felt like a poke in the eye to the southern cause.

This document proclaimed that all slaves in the Confederate states were to be freed. We had to laugh at this since Missouri and the other border states in rebellion were exempt and Lincoln had only freed slaves in those areas that did not recognize the Federal government. He had also energized the radical abolitionists by changing the focus of the war from that of preserving his blessed Union to the liberation of our slaves.

Closer to home Vicksburg, Mississippi, the city we called the 'Gibraltar of the Confederacy,' was under siege by that general named U. S. Grant. The Mississippi River was now open to Federal gunboats since the once feared batteries on the Vicksburg bluffs no longer posed a threat. I had heard that Jacob had volunteered to serve in what I guess you could call the Confederate Navy and was serving somewhere in Mississippi, so he was in the thick of it.

Not everything in the Trans-Mississippi (such was called the theater of war west of the Mississippi River) was as bleak for our cause as it might seem, however. Earlier in the year the veteran of Boonville and now a general, John Sappington Marmaduke, whose father had been a Missouri governor before the war (who knew that after the war he would follow in his father's footsteps?), had made a successful raid into Missouri and burned the Springfield Supply Depot. This raid energized our guerilla bands in the area and made life a living hell for the Yankees for a time.

My brother Guffey had been involved in the Springfield victory and had been promoted to sergeant. I was happy for him but I was starting to enjoy my role as an 'irregular' soldier in my personal war with the occupying bastards.

Since becoming a fugitive, of course, I also encountered many men of questionable character. I remember my grandfather saying that 'politics make strange bed fellows' and that was never truer than for me. My current situation dictated that I suspend a great deal of the moral teachings I learned at my father's knee. I had been thoroughly schooled in the precepts of the Holy Bible and the Episcopal Book of Common Prayer, but they were of no consequence to me now. The simple lessons of those timeless sources of wisdom were now overshadowed by the brutal realities of war. My Pa was rotting in the Glasgow jail, the family homestead burned, the livestock long ago stolen and all the wealth that my father and the members of our extended family had worked so hard to accumulate had gone up in smoke along with the buildings.

My mother and aunt and all the younger children were living in exile, hidden by family and friendly supporters in Rocheport. My cousin was somewhere in the Confederate Navy and I had not a clue as to his well being.

And what about me? At the risk of sounding sorry for myself I must say that I had become a mere shadow of my former self. I'd been on the run living mostly by the charity of supporters of the Confederate cause. These brave men and women had risked everything to hide, feed and clothe me and my fellow partisans who were hunted like beasts by the hated Yankee dogs.

All this is to say that I had been for some time running with a rough crowd and was the worse for wear from it. Some, like me, had been thrust into this life by circumstances beyond their control. Others were no better than thugs and outlaws. Yet necessity dictated what the old saying proclaimed, 'we must hang together or be hung separately.' This was a literal truth.

At eighteen I thought I had encountered all that was evil in the world. I had been so naïve. I had just joined up with the devil incarnate and God help me, I was proud of that devil, 'Bloody Bill' Anderson. Anderson's story was a sad one, like most of us. In one way or another our boys had somehow been able to hold on to a modicum of sanity. I mean to say, most of our boys. But not Anderson or some of his original followers like George Todd and Arch Clement. Everyone said that like me, Anderson had been somewhat "bookish" as a young man. How things had changed.

One evening, following a successful but uneventful raid on a militia camp near Independence, we were sitting around a campfire spinning yarns. The conversation turned to stories about our leader.

My lanky new friend Alexander Franklin James was three or four years older than me but had seen lots of action with Quantrill, especially on the Lawrence raids, and he filled us in on some of the lesser known facts about Bill Anderson. Frank said that his family had seen hard times on the Prairie and even though they had acquired land, a store by the Santa Fe Trail and a substantial net worth, fate struck them a devastating blow. Their Ma, who was only in her mid 30's, was struck by lightning and killed, leaving behind six children, the youngest only a year old.

Bill, the oldest son, had a good reputation in the area and at age 21 staked his own claim. But then rumors and suspicions arose regarding his activities involving questionable horse trading. The coming of the war did not seem to hamper the Anderson's business. In fact, it probably enhanced it as they became the full time Kansas bandits we came to call Jayhawkers.

In 1861 forays into Missouri by Jayhawking Kansans under the guise of freeing slaves and punishing the rebellious Missourians was so great that the Governor declared that the state was 'overrun with thieves and highway robbers.'

We objected to Frank calling Bill a Jayhawker, but he said that the Andersons had always held southern sentiments and that their Jayhawking was strictly for financial gain. Politics aside, the real trouble began when a judge living near Council Grove, Kansas, on the Santa Fe Trail, had gunned down Jim and Bill Anderson's father, William, after accusing his cousin of horse stealing. The authorities also believed that the Anderson brothers were involved in their cousins activities as well. Bill was arrested but released on bond much to the dismay of the judge who wanted him to be lynched on the spot. The boys fled to Johnson County, Kansas, in the hope that things would cool down. They changed their minds, though, and a couple of months later the Anderson brothers and two of their friends returned to the judge's home and killed him and his sixteen year old brother-in-law. Bill's brother, Jim, was shot in the thigh in the melee. But it was not a serious wound and the exuberant party returned to Lafayette County, Missouri.

Subsequently, the death and injuries to his sisters provided the spark that inflamed his quest for revenge. I certainly could relate. Yes, I had become sympathetic to the cause of freedom and states rights, a movement that was so dear to my family, friends and neighbors, but my primary cause now was revenge. It was not yet satisfied, even after I had brought justice to the lowlife Yankee Dutch bastards who had raped my friend and tutor, but that was what started me down this terrible road to perdition. And now there was the matter of freeing my pa from incarceration and settling up with Wyllis R. Curtis.

Curtis was now a judge and a Colonel in the Union militia. While growing up, I had known the Curtis family. They had several children about my age but I never cared for them. They lived on a hard scrabble farm not far from Fayette and for reasons never known to me, old man Curtis had it in for my father. The youngsters were poorly educated and downright mean. I swear that they stole from us and others continuously until Pa had a hard talk with Curtis. Politics being what they are, Curtis became a rising star in the new Republican party and in spite or because of his fundamental ignorance was appointed judge, holding court in Fayette.

After the occupation of Howard County, he was elected Colonel of the local military establishment and fanatically set out to rid the neighborhood of any southern sympathizers, especially those with wealth. His patriotic frenzy was mostly fueled by greed. The war provided him an avenue for upward mobility and prestige that he had never dreamed of prior to Mr. Lincoln's election.

Curtis was the man responsible for my family's troubles. He was the man who personally arrested my Pa and told his troops to torch our homestead. I wasn't sure how, but somehow I was going to free my father from his prison cell and look at Colonel Wyllis R. Curtis with my cold steely eyes as I discharged my beloved Navy Colts into his large belly.

Chapter Twelve

In the summer of 1863 Brigadier General Thomas Ewing, Jr., the brother-in-law of that sonofabitch Yankee General William Sherman, was the head Federal in these parts when our partisan leader William Quantrill and some of his raiders ambushed a patrol, killing fourteen of the hated Yankees. This incensed the General who decided to punish the guerrillas through the time honored Federal practice of charging family, friends and sympathizers of aiding and abetting. Sound familiar? Hence the imprisonment and subsequent tragic fate, mentioned earlier.

Well, there was no stopping Anderson's rage now! The death and maiming of his sisters made financial gain secondary. To kill and terrorize anyone, civilian or soldier who supported the Union, became his reason to be.

I must admit, however, that even though our obsession for revenge was indeed our primary motive, we did not hesitate to help ourselves to the Yankee treasures along the way. In fact, I was getting rich from my share of the take. I had never seen so much coin of the realm. My conscience was clear on this plundering business. Hell, the Federals had taken everything from us. Turn about is only fair play. Grandma often said "What's good for the goose is good for the gander." Thank God she passed before all this came to be.

This was the man I now righteously served. His band of bushwhackers provided me with a sense of relative security and if I had to kill some of the blue coated bastards along the way that was fine with me. And since we were living and raiding in familiar territory I figured I could inflict some of my personal revenge upon a certain individual in Howard County. The sonofabitch that had wrongfully placed my Pa in prison and had burned my ancestral home was dead. He just didn't know it! Like 'Bloody Bill,' the war, my war, continued to be fed by a growing number of personal grievances. Politics be damned!

Before I tell you about my efforts to get to my Pa in hopes of freeing him from the Glasgow jail, I feel it only fitting to give a little background on what I had been up to in the meantime. John McCorkle was a Howard County boy like myself. Like most everyone, his family had settled in the county and loved his life there. Our county government was an old one since it had been formed by the territorial legislature way back in 1816. Folks called it 'the mother of all counties' since thirty-nine counties were spawned from the original. But the occupation changed everything, and the McCorkle family pulled up stakes and moved to Jackson County hoping to build a better life.

In April of 1861, following the untimely death of his father, John enlisted along with many of his young neighbors in Company A of the Missouri State Guard, eventually drilling in Independence.

Following a few deadly skirmishes with some Union forces sent from Kansas City, his unit was ordered to disband and return to their homes. It wasn't long, though, before they received orders to join our own General Price on his march toward Lexington. After that successful engagement, his unit followed Price's army south, but John became seriously ill with what we called 'camp fever', a flu-like condition eventually identified as Typhus, and spread by lice. He ended up recuperating at his mother's home back in Jackson County. John was still suffering when his Confederate sympathizing family was threatened by followers of Jim Lane and the red leg Jennison. These Jayhawkers prompted John to rejoin the cause. Near Springfield he and some other recruits were captured by the Federals. After some time in confinement he took the oath of allegiance and was paroled. Back in Jackson County he and the others who had previously served the southern cause were treated badly and robbed of most of their belongings. Besides, even after swearing the oath, these men were still subject to imprisonment or death.

In an effort to avoid the Federal militia he hightailed it as fast as he could. And that's when fate took charge of his life and led him into mine.

I had been living as best I could off the generosity
of my friends and neighbors but it had been a hard
winter for me. Yankee patrols were everywhere and
close calls became the norm. I thought I was a goner
back in February of that year when I was staying at
the home of Mr. Davis and his wife, who, by the way,
was the finest cook I had ever known, bar none.

Early one morning there was a ruckus out in the
yard when a squad of militia out of Independence
rode up and started yelling at Mr. Davis who had just
returned from milking. They demanded breakfast,
and stomped into the parlor, muddy boots and all.
Mrs. Davis fixed their breakfast and I stayed upstairs
with Mr. Davis' shotgun and my Navy Colts at the
ready. The soldiers were extremely loud and rude
and at one time I was almost compelled to storm
down and silence their profanity once and for all, but
common sense prevailed, at least on that occasion.

Weeks later, I was hiding with the George Wiggington family near Independence. This time, due to
the beautiful spring weather and the equally pleasant company of Miss Molly Wiggington I darn near
forgot that I was a fugitive being hunted by the Yankee occupiers. On such a day several riders approached the farm and tethered their mounts to the
front yard fence. As I peered from the barn I was
pleasantly surprised when Mr. Wiggington waved me
out of hiding and into the presence of my old friend
from home, John McCorkle.

John told us he had attempted to abide by his

parole, but he had finally had enough. The Jackson
County Federals had threatened to toss him into a
dungeon unless he could make a bond of $5,000.
His crime? He had been hauled before the court for
singing. Someone had heard him singing a rebel
song. Having neither the inclination to surrender
nor, for that matter, $5,000, John hightailed it from
his mother's farm under cover of darkness.

The first step on his journey into exile was his
call on Uncle George. John told him that he just
couldn't take it any longer. Over another spectacular
supper lovingly prepared by his aunt, John let the
hurt and frustration he felt explode upon the gathering. He had honestly and conscientiously believed in
the principles of the Confederacy. He affirmed his
belief in states rights and his desire to join the
cause. Sickness had intervened and then capture
before he had even been issued a weapon. Finally,
he had then taken the Yankee oath and had intended
to abide by it. But that was then.

At the ripe old age of 22 he could no longer toler-
ate what was happening. I asked him what he intended to do. John looked at me with cold eyes and
proclaimed that he was on his way to meet up with
his friends from Lone Jack and join the notorious
colonel, William Quantrill. I already knew that a partisan group was holed up at Lone Jack that was
headed by John Little. Sam Montgomery and Dick
Hopkins were there as well. Quantrill was just more
good news.

"I'm going with you John," I said, "My cause is your cause. Welcome to the family."

Up until now I have belabored the facts that led up to how a bunch of law abiding farm boys turned into fledgling bushwhackers. So it would seem somewhat appropriate to at least give a smattering of background on the fellow that aided me in my quest for revenge and damn near got me killed on more than one occasion.

William Clark Quantrill was born in Maryland but as a young man sought his fortune on the wild frontier. Not far from the free state town of Lawrence, Kansas, Quantrill alleged that a band of red legged Jayhawkers had killed his 18-year-old brother and wounded him in the leg. Believing both boys to be dead, the Kansans made off with Quantrill's wagon and mules, all their provisions and two Negroes who had been helping them. Somehow, with the help of an Indian who discovered him out on the prairie, William survived. The birth of his hate occurred that day and from that moment on the bile of revenge was never far from his throat.

Some have said he made this story up in order to justify his actions. I couldn't say, but I do know first hand that he wasn't partial to Kansans.

Quantrill was living in Missouri when the war began. At first he attempted to assist the Federal authorities as they tried to deal with the continued lawlessness perpetrated by the Jayhawkers. But then an incident occurred where Quantrill and a small band of his followers were fired upon by Federal soldiers. This was a big mistake by the boys in blue since return fire killed five men in the first volley. Following this incident considerable time and energy was spent by the Yankees trying to capture the men who had not started the fight. As a wanted man, Quantrill now directed his energies to the southern cause and raised a call for men to join him in this endeavor.

*   *   *

Early the next morning George Wiggington, John McCorkle and I mounted our horses and headed to the camp of Cole Younger. After a week there we received word that we should meet up with Quantrill the following Sunday at Blue Springs. I was very excited about meeting the man who was the center of all the ruckus.

I met him, but didn't get to speak to him since there were about sixty of us from Lone Jack along with 350 Confederate partisans from all over the county. All together, this was a rag-tag band of raw recruits with a smattering of old soldiers trying to keep order. I thanked the Lord that I had been in the Howard County militia and at least knew a little something about soldiering.

The plan was to attack the Federals at the court house in Independence. Colonel Hughes was to command this operation. A great cloud of dust rose behind us so we had to forego the element of surprise. We received fire from the bank and the court house and several of our men were wounded in the first volley. A fellow I had shared coffee with earlier that same morning took a shot in the foot. As I bent down to help him remove his boot a slug passed about an inch from my left ear, and oddly, for the first time I realized this war was for real. I was no longer fantasizing about the hell I would bring to the Yankee bastards who had wronged me and mine. That hell was now descending on me in the form of .57 caliber minie balls. I hate to admit it, but I pissed my pants. Smoke and dust were everywhere. There was nothing for me to shoot for the enemy was in hiding and I was out of ammunition. Somehow this initial panic passed and I regained control of my emotions.

Off to my right some tents had been pitched in a field so I headed there to see what I could find. The Feds had skedaddled, leaving some bacon still frying on the fire and equally important to me, a box of ammunition not far away. Several of our party had accompanied me and we filled our pouches with powder and shot and our cheeks with the finest bacon I had ever tasted. In retrospect, the bacon probably wasn't all that different, but the circumstances heightened my taste buds. Leaving our horses at the tents, we headed back toward the fighting going on outside the buildings.

Some Federal soldiers who must have been from

the camp we had just raided were crouching behind a rock fence. I figured they must have run from the tents since I could see several were still in their underwear. Unfortunately for us, though, they had the presence of mind to take their Springfield rifles with them. We only had shotguns and Navy pistols that were useless at this range.

Our other leader, Colonel Hayes, asked for volunteers to slip around behind the rock fence through a sweet potato patch and try to drive the defenders out in the open. Barney Chambers, a Presbyterian minister and the bravest man I had ever seen headed out with about thirty men. I tagged along since I didn't want to appear cowardly. In a matter of minutes we were pelted with a hailstorm of minie balls. No one was hit, except the reverend, who was shredded to pieces. I guess according to the reverend's religion it had been predestined to happen that way, but I think it was a real shame.

The long and short of it is that we retreated back to our horses. Colonel Quantrill and his men stormed down the road toward the court house. They had just finished routing a detachment on the Kansas City road. Sizing up the situation, he ordered men to set fire to the court house as a steady stream of lead was sent toward the windows. It was not long before a white flag fluttered and the garrison surrendered. The prisoners were formed into ranks on the court house square, disarmed and paroled. Two farmers who had been jailed as southern supporters, and who had been scheduled for execution, were freed. We then helped ourselves to all of the Federal supplies that we could carry and triumphantly headed back to Blue Springs.

The next day our newly formed company of 120 men was sworn into the service of the Confederacy under the auspices of the Partisan Ranger Act of 1862. I was as happy as I had been in years. The personal cause I had been waging was now validated in this even greater cause. And life in the camp at Blue Springs was good, but our idleness was not for long.

Word came that the hated Kansan Colonel Hoyt and his red-legged Jayhawkers were headed on a mission to burn Independence. This seemed strange to me, since Independence was home to Yankees, but what did I know? Ironically, some of us were sent to be pickets on the Kansas City - Independence Road, but Hoyt never came. So we headed back just in time to discover we had missed the battle of Lone Jack where, on August 15th, a Union force of about 800 men under the command of a Major Foster met up with Confederate Commander Colonel John Coffee and 1,200 men. The Federals had laid a thorny, impenetrable hedge of bois d'arc trees out in front of their position. They also had a battery of two cannons that apparently caused a great deal of damage to our Confederate attackers. The main street of Lone Jack resembled a street in hell for a while, but in the end our force prevailed and the crippled Yankees limped back to safety in Lexington. Altogether, 55 of our boys were killed that day. Losses were much higher for the enemy, but I did not know the exact number of fatalities they suffered.

The Federals had run roughshod over the Confederate sympathizers ever since the conflict began, including my family, and with indignities too numerous to mention.

One good example of how things were can be illustrated by my involvement with a man whose deeds turned my stomach inside out. His name was Levi Copeland. This free-state loving Lieutenant was captured at Lone Jack. Copeland had been searching for two boys that served in my unit. One day he went to their father's farm and demanded that he tell him their whereabouts. Their father said nothing. Copeland then had his henchmen drag the old man to a tree in their yard and in front of his wife and daughters had him hanged.

Quantrill had heard of the incident, and after some haggling with the colonel who had Copeland in custody ordered John, George and myself to go fetch the bastard. We delivered the lieutenant as directed. Quantrill questioned him for a bit and then turned him over to the old man's sons. They promptly led him into the woods and he was never heard of again.

We camped at Lone Jack for a time, making a few unsuccessful raids over by the Little Blue River, but the Federals were now as thick as fleas on a hound dog, so Colonel Quantrill ordered us to disband for

Billy's War
the time being.

Chapter Thirteen

This chronicle of my activities with Quantrill, Anderson and the band of wild and reckless teenagers seems far back in the distant past, but it was only a year since I'd last seen my home. At any rate, it was now time for me to head to Glasgow and set my Pa free.

I had to travel at night, but I knew the area well. I also knew the farms that would gladly provide me with sanctuary and I hopscotched my way from Lone Jack to Odessa to Waverly, where I was able to catch a ferry across the river without raising any suspicion. At Salisbury I stayed a couple of days at the home of Mr. Cummins and his family, a prosperous farmer and secret supporter of our cause,. The morning of the third day I was being treated to breakfast when a Negro came to the house reporting that a company of Federals was camped in the creek bottom just about a mile away.

This news curbed my appetite so I apologized to Mrs. Cummins for leaving in the middle of my biscuits and gravy and made my escape. Normally I did not venture out during the daylight, but necessity is the mother of invention. My horse was fresh and strong and it was not long before the Yankee threat was long behind me.

I had been given the name of another secesh family who lived on a farm north of Glasgow on the Salsbury road. Finding no enemy in the vicinity, I approached the house where I was warmly but tentatively received. After explaining my mission, the elderly gentleman went to a cabinet and poured us a couple of full glasses of corn liquor from a demijohn. After riding for so long with bushwhackers and hard cases I had acquired somewhat of a taste for hard liquor, at least for the effect it created in my mind, if not really for the taste. It was a cold night and I welcomed this family's hospitality. We toasted General Price and my father's old friend Governor Claiborne Jackson.

I settled back, letting the harsh burning liquid settle over me. I suggested that we should also drink to my new found hero, Colonel William Quantrill. My host poured three fingers of the drug into our glasses and we drank them down. The roaring fire in the parlor fireplace coupled with the rapidly spreading effects of the corn whiskey settled over me like my grandmother's quilt. I felt a moment's peace. And then the old man told me the news I both needed and dreaded to hear..

It seems that my father, Durette Henry Peyton, had languished in the county jail since he was arrested. Normally, suspected secessionists were dealt with in a timely fashion, often without a trial, fair or otherwise. Usually they were merely strung from the nearest tree or shot and left to rot by the side of the road.

But since my father was of some prominence in the community, the Federal authorities had walked on eggs for over a year. Finally, the military court, fed by the damning testimony of Colonel Wyllis Curtis, declared that my father was a traitor and he was sentenced to hang. The blood drained from my face as I listened to this account. A few moments ago I had been warm and cozy, now I was ice cold.

I raised my hand and reminded my drinking companion that I had known of my father's imprisonment and this was the reason I was sharing these moments of hospitality with him and his family. I had come to break Pa out or die trying. I drained my glass in anticipation of this upcoming challenge.

The old man stood and walking toward the fire, blurted sadly, "It ain't going to do you no good. Your Pa's dead. But damned if he didn't cheat the gallows. He died from pneumonia four days ago." My blood ran cold. I had come too late!

There was no reason for me to endanger these good people any longer. I left at first light feeling a great need to visit my home place over in Howard County. My heart was heavy with sadness and things were not made better by the pounding headache I attributed to the liquid fire I had consumed last evening. There was no safe harbor for me around Fayette, so I spent the next night tucked reasonably comfortably in a shallow cave I had played in not that many years ago. The next day I was cold and hungry as I rode up the lane, past the cemetery of my ancestors.

Nothing remained, only the skeletons of chimneys in the main house. I was overcome with emotions. Sadness to the verge of tears was replaced with an anger greater than I had ever experienced. And believe me, I had experienced anger.

It was not safe for me to linger, so I set out across the land, knowing that the God Damned Feds would only travel the roads. My destination was the secessionist friendly town of Rocheport. I knew that I would find safety there as I formulated my plans for revenge.

It was a bittersweet reunion with my mother and all my kin. I was happy to see them since I had been away so long, but it was difficult to see the sad state of affairs their lives had become. The family was scattered out among several distant cousins who had willingly taken them, but times were so very hard. My Aunt Sophie was skin and bones and longed only for news of her son Jacob. A pall of sorrow hung over my loved ones. Pa was gone and the awful news had drifted in that my little brother Guffey had died of smallpox while serving down near Batesville, Arkansas.

To top everything off, the hardship of my travels and exposure to the elements had finally taken their toll, and I went down. Though nearly succumbing to the pneumonia myself, the excellent nursing of my sisters and the superb medical knowledge of my mother spared me from my father's fate.

No one had knowledge of where or what George William was about. Some of my kin believed that he had joined up with the regular Federal army and had gone out east, but the thought of that happening just stuck in my craw. The best news was that Miss Milly and the Yates family had been spared much of the misery we had experienced.

And so the winter passed. As my health improved I was able to assist with the chores and even venture from the farm on a few occasions. The news from out east was not encouraging especially after the fall of Vicksburg.

Now and then some of my partisan friends would ride out with the latest news. Colonel Quantrill's escapades continued to harass the Feds and news of his exploits, especially his raid on Lawrence, Kansas, gave me hope and inspired me to recovery.

By spring I had regained my health and was rearing to spring vengeance on the dastardly Colonel Wyllis Curtis, whose activities I had been monitoring with increased interest. I learned that most days he would be escorted from a fine house he had stolen, although the Federals used the word 'confiscated' or 'appropriated,' from a family who had championed the Southern cause. His escort consisted of a fancy-rigged three-man squad. The pompous Colonel Curtis, who did not hold a commission in the regular army, only the state guard, had adorned himself with the most elaborate uniform money could buy. His hat was adorned with a black ostrich feather and his buggy and horse were equipped with the finest tack shipped to him from New Orleans.

Now mind you that before the war this illiterate sonofabitch could barely scratch out a living for himself and his mean-spirited children. I was itching for a fight, but I had no desire to stage a suicide mission.

One beautiful late spring day I was pleasantly surprised by a visit from John McCorkle, George Wiggington and our old friends and fellow Bushwhackers Sam Montgomery and Dick Hopkins. The boys had been given permission to return to their homes for the winter. They had taken this round about way back to Jackson County and duty with Colonel Quantrill just to see me and find out how I was doing.

After staying with us for a few days rest, George, who was the oldest and the natural leader, said that they needed to leave soon. That is when I explained my need to send the good Colonel Curtis to hell, and how their assistance in this endeavor would please me to no end. Everyone agreed that it would be an appropriate send off for us, since I had made up my mind to accompany them back to the ongoing fight in Jackson County.

The next evening we set out on reconnaissance.

Just as I had been told, the party came trotting down the highway in regal splendor. Before the turn off to the lane leading up to his fine brick house there was a draw that crossed a shallow creek.

There was a steep bank on the right side of the road and a marsh on the left. George suggested this would be an excellent location for an ambush and we all agreed.

We learned the escort was armed with Sharps carbines, but they were encased in saddle holsters. We didn't know what, if any, weapon Curtis carried, but we believed the element of surprise would compensate for any of our shortcomings. This strategy had worked successfully many times in my bushwhacking career and I had no fear that we would experience another victory. I could hardly stand the wait. I hated this man with, as the prayer says though not in this context, "all my heart and soul and mind."

Back at the Rocheport farm we collected and readied our weapons. Everyone had at least two Navy colts and George and Dick Hopkins augmented their arsenals with 12-guage shotguns. Though the waiting was excruciating, we opted to execute our attack in the evening when the party was returning home in the belief that they would be less alert.

I implemented one addition to the plan that I was sure would insure success. Just before the Yankees left Fayette we drove a team with a large farm wagon that we 'borrowed' from a Union neighbor and placed

the wagon sideways in the dip of the road. No sooner
had George led the team into the surrounding woods
than we heard the buggy and its precious bodyguard
in the distance. I prayed that no one would come
along to complicate matters, and thankfully no one
came.

When the Federals turned toward the lane we
slipped out of the woods and followed the horsemen,
staying about thirty yards behind them in the dust.
Then as the buggy headed down into the draw we
spurred our horses and charged the unsuspecting
Yanks. We labored under no code of chivalry.

George and Dick galloped within feet of the rear
guard when one of the Federals, who looked to be
about my age, glanced back just in time to see
George crack him across his body with the stock of
his shotgun. The horses reared and another man
was mercilessly thrown from his horse. One more
rider remained. He was mine. Armed with both
Navy colts I emptied them as he frantically attempted
to control his mount. But damn it all, I missed. His
horse helped me, though, and he was thrown face
down into the dusty road.

Ahead of them Curtis had stopped the buggy and
was cussing the fool who had blocked the road with
the wagon. Before he could say more, George busted
him with the shotgun butt so hard that it knocked
him to the floor of the buggy. This startled his horse
who bolted and dumped his passenger into the muck
and ooze of the marsh.

The wounded Federal that George had hit took off back down the road as fast as he could. I shouted to let him go since we had greater fish to fry. Poor Wyllis, dazed and bloody and sitting upright in the bog finally came to his senses. And then he saw me. There was no misunderstanding the terror that overcame him.

George and Dick had collected our remaining prisoners. They also gathered up the prized Sharps rifles and were wrapping them in their sleeping blankets.

The cocky Colonel didn't look quite as regal as he had a few minutes before. I told him to get up and take it like a man. But he stayed in the mud and began to beg like the coward he was. My Colts were empty so I asked George if I could have his for just a moment.

"I'll give it right back to you, George, I won't need it for very long," I said.

George handed it over, saying,

"Be my guest. It's the best use of lead I've seen in a long time!"

Old man Curtis continued to plead and babble something about how sorry he was and that he didn't mean for all this misery to happen to my family. It was everyone's fault but his. He would make everything better, he pled.

And then Dick shot one of our captive soldiers with his shotgun, blowing parts of his innards all over the mighty Colonel. This act reduced Curtis to

a squalling, retching, sorry excuse for a human being.

"Get up," I yelled. This time he complied.

"Go to hell, you bastard," were the last words he
heard as I placed one shot in his gut and another in
the top of his head as he doubled over. We let the
remaining guard go, the lucky sonofabitch who had
somehow escaped the 12 shots from my Navys. I
told him to walk to the main house and tell all that
he had seen and heard. I also told him that no Yankee loving sonofabitch was safe and that Billy Peyton
and William Quantrill were getting ready to burn
Fayette to the ground.

Having made this fanciful boast, I mounted and
we rode off down the Fayette Road.

Chapter Fourteen

It didn't take long for the alarm to sound and send the Bluecoats swarming as thick as thieves, but we disappeared into a secret bushwhacker hideout up in the wilderness area of Howard county called the Perche Hills. No Yankee had ever dared to venture into this rugged landscape. It had been home to partisans since the war started and a haven for outlaws prior to that.

The newspapers had a heyday with the story and for a brief time my name was spread across the headlines as the most recent Confederate scoundrel. The article I read in the Boonville paper in fact made me out to be a bloodthirsty raider. Of course there was no mention as to why this revenge action had been perpetrated by William Peyton, formerly of Howard County.

We camped out in the Perche hideout for a couple of weeks, venturing out only to steal a few Yankee chickens and a horse or two. On one trip, George stopped a stage coach and relieved the passengers of their valuables and several quarts of very good whiskey. Of course we made sure that the contributors were Union men, as we would never take from one they now called a "secech."

After things settled down and the militia went back to the safety of their barracks, we headed to the Rocheport farm for baths, clean clothing and a home cooked meal. It was now time for us to leave the Boone's Lick area and head back to our Jackson County command. John and Sam decided to visit relatives up in Randolph County and left the day before we did, vowing to meet up again at our partisan camp. After leaving hearth and home I foolishly decided to celebrate and attend a barn dance that was being held in the German community near Rocheport.

These Dutch had been industrious people and good neighbors as well as trading partners before the war. But they were staunchly Union men and had caused a great deal of misery for us since the war started. It was a little dangerous to mingle in the midst of what was now a hostile population, but we figured there would be enough people there that we wouldn't be noticed. As it turned out, this wasn't exactly the case.

On the way to the dance we had passed a bottle of liberated whiskey between us and were in high spirits when we arrived. Out of habit, we tethered our mounts on the edge of the woods and joined the throng. There were some pretty girls in attendance but none would give us the time of day, let alone a place on their dance cards. We split up as George and Dick headed for the table of food. Unfortunately, and against my better judgment, I sampled a cup of delicious hard cider and then another and yes, one more. The music was fine and everyone was in gay spirits; well, everyone but me. The happiness and good will that had accompanied me to the event was now slipping away, no doubt attributable to the quantity of drink I had consumed. Something about these prosperous goddamned Dutch who showed no sign of suffering due to the war just rankled me. They still had it all and we had nothing. Seeing trouble brewing, George and Dick slipped away and headed for the safety of Jackson County. To this day, I don't know what came over me, but I commenced to do one of the most stupid things I have ever done. And I do believe I have done a few. I boldly marched up to this big fat Dutchman who played very well, I admit it. But I looked into his rosy cheeked well fed face and shouted over the din of the crowd,

"If I couldn't play the fiddle any better than that, I'd break it!"

So what does he do? He hands the fiddle to me. What a fool I am, I can't play the fiddle. Lots of people were staring at me by now. So I did the only thing I could do. I broke it and ran like hell for my horse. It must have been half the county that took off after me and cut me off from the only road to escape. I faced the Missouri River at my back and an ever growing crowd of hostile Germans in front. I had no choice. Into the river Blackey and I went,

and believe you me I was instantly sober. I had
forded some creeks on my horse before, but never
the treacherous, spring rain-gorged mighty Missouri.

Hanging on to my poor horse's tail I looked back
at the shore filled with my cursing neighbors and
knew that if I made it across the river it would be a
very long time before I would be welcome back in
that German community near Rocheport.

How stupid could anyone get? I had experienced
so much hate and discontent in my young life. and I
had slipped through some mighty tight spots. But
this predicament was of my own making. I had been
relatively safe and certainly comfortable before that
ill fated barn dance, but my foolishly conceived bra-
vado, fueled by some of the finest Dutch cider and
corn whiskey had certainly led me astray. Any way,
Blackey and his foolish rider eventually found ourselves on the opposite bank.

Wet and cold in hostile country since Boonville
had surrendered to Yankee occupation at the very
beginning of our Missouri war, I was at a loss as to
how to proceed. I knew I couldn't just stay in the
woods and catch pneumonia again, so I led my horse
through the bottoms until I found a trail leading east
toward Columbia. Oh, Columbia! How I had
dreamed of attending the University, studying law,
surrounded by my fellows arguing the finer points of
the profession over cheap beer in the local establishments. Instead, here I was, sloshing along, freez-
ing my ass off with not a clue as to what fate might

bring. And, it was all my own damn fault. That was the worst part. There was no one to blame but myself.

This self recrimination brought me to the verge of tears. My self loathing mixed with a good dose of self pity had cast a debilitating pall over my normal self suffering and positive countenance.

Then, as I trudged over a small knoll, I spotted the dark silhouettes of outbuildings. A spark of hope hit me like a lightning bolt. I can't remember having a rush of hope as powerful as I experienced at that moment. I quickly unsaddled my horse and tethered him back in the woods. A shiver of cold spread through my body, more from excitement than the numbing cold of my soaked clothing.

Taking my saddle bag with its precious cargo of Yankee money and my Navy colts I quietly approached the first structure, which turned out to be a very large and substantially built barn. It had been painted red, which telegraphed to the community that the property belonged to Missourians of German extraction and therefore more than likely supporters of Uncle Abe's Union. This didn't worry me much but the prospect of a pack of dogs discovering my presence and alerting the occupants of the house did. Luckily I made it to the barn without incident. It was darker inside than out and not much warmer. I felt my way through the cavernous interior. There was a stirring of the animals inside but nothing that would alert the household.

A small room was located near the front door, and I went in. As my eyes adjusted to the darkness I spotted a small desk and chair against the far wall. Hanging on a peg next to the glassed in window was an old pair of overalls and a worn jacket.

The finest apparel from St. Louis or New Orleans could not have made me happier. Quickly I shucked my sodden clothing and experienced the blessed warmth of my new outfit. After a few moments of this new found bliss, I spread my gear out to dry and fumbled in the dark for my pistols. Fortunately the powder flasks and caps had remained sealed and dry. I found a rag and carefully dried my Colts. I then loaded them and headed back into the interior of the barn. I discovered a ladder leading to the loft and up I went. I placed my colts on the floor before me and dived deep into the warmth of the hay.

This was certainly not the first time I had hidden in a barn, but it was by far the best.

The next thing I knew a stream of sunlight was flooding my face through a crack in the wall. I jolted awake, forgetting for a moment where I was and the circumstances that had brought me here. It didn't take long, however, to come to the present. There was a commotion outside in the lane so I jumped to the loft door, expecting the worst.

Instead of a regiment of Yankees hell bent on hanging me from the nearest tree, I witnessed several children excitedly leading my horse toward the house. Blackey had slipped his tether and had wandered, like me, towards the possibility of food and shelter. The house was much closer than I had thought and I had a clear view of the proceedings. After a moment, it occurred to me that it wasn't prudent to remain a spectator.

I picked up my pistols and headed down the ladder and out the far side of the barn. I was barefoot but farm boys are used to not wearing shoes. I slipped behind the house whose occupants had gathered around my horse. Everyone was excited and babbling in their foreign tongue. I knew it wouldn't be long before someone would be sent to raise the alarm with the local militia, so I boldly stepped out from my hiding place and started walking toward the gathered spectators.

A boy of about ten spotted me first. I must have been quite a sight, wearing his Pa's oversized clothing. I had tucked the Colts in the coat pockets, but I'm sure I startled the entire group. It was a large family, mother and father, with a gaggle of children ranging from early teens to a babe in arms. I raised my hands in the universal symbol of friendship. The Dutchman stepped forward and I opened the conversation.

"Speak English?"

"Ya, what do you want?"

I figured there was no harm in telling the truth, at least some of it. I said I was a partisan ranger on the run and that I was cold and hungry and would hurt no one if they would do as I say.

The head of the household turned to his family and barked some orders in crisp German. Turning back to me he said,

"We wish you no harm. I am a farmer, not a politician. I have seen too much war back in the old country and I do not want it here. You are safe, come inside."

The stove was already on and the kitchen smells caused a violent contraction in my stomach. It was not long before biscuits and gravy and a heaping mound of bacon were placed before me. It was almost like I was some sort of honored guest. But I kept a wary eye on the whole family lest someone decided to tuck and run. I didn't need to point out to my hosts that their hospitality could get them in a heap of trouble with the local authorities. Harboring a Confederate was a serious offense even in Boone County.

The boys fed and watered my horse and fetched my saddle gear. The girls brought my damp clothing to the house where the Missus dried them by the fire and even ironed them crisp. The only time I showed my weapons was when I changed clothes. I learned that this man's name was Heinrich Yeager.

By noon I was ready to head out. I packed my belongings as the children saddled my horse. I thanked them for the shelter they had provided me and offered a small poke of money. Mr. Yeager declined this offer, but as his wife handed me a sack of bacon and biscuits I slipped her a $5 gold piece which she shyly pocketed in her apron. I asked for directions to Columbia and headed toward the main road. My departure was heralded by a chorus of goodbyes from the Yeager children.

When I reached the main road I headed away from Columbia and back toward Boonville. I knew that the good and honest Mr. Yeager would inform the militia if asked about my visit and intended destination.

I skirted the town of Boonville and arrived at a small ferry I had used before just about dark. A young boy and his father carried me and Blackey across the Missouri River certainly in greater comfort than the last time we were there. The ferryman was a supporter of the cause and would not alert the authorities. Back safely in Howard County, I struck out to a house in Franklin that I knew would provide me safe harbor.

The Widow Hawkins had assisted our partisans from the very beginning of the Yankee occupation. Her husband had been killed early on at the battle of Carthage, and she harbored no good will for the Union oppressors. Mrs. Hawkins had avoided Yankee suspicion however, since she had outwardly welcomed and supported the Union cause and those who enforced it. To the 'loyal' public, she was a paragon of patriotic virtue, helping the local auxiliary of the Baptist church host social functions and openly denouncing Confederate supporters. Behind the scenes she had learned from the Yankees how to run an underground railroad of her own.

Her house was safely located away from the main road to Franklin and was surrounded by a dense forest. If the coast was clear she would hang a water bucket on the pump. Horses could be hidden in a deep ravine about a hundred yards behind the barn and so far, not one of the local citizens was aware of her true vocation.

It was after dark when I reached the Hawkins place. I left my horse in the woods and to my delight discovered that the water bucket was in full view. A light flickered in the parlor and I slipped up and peeked in the window. It appeared that Mrs. Hawkins was alone. I had met her before but had never needed her assistance. She was a beautiful woman in her mid twenties with flaming red hair neatly arranged in the fashion of the day.

For a moment I felt ashamed of my peeking Tom behavior, but rationalized it as simply being cautious. I didn't want to frighten her with my sudden appearance so I went back to my horse and rode up to the front door. A dinner bell hung from a post and I carefully hit the clapper. Within seconds the light dimmed and I could feel her eyes on me. I yelled,

"It's Billy. Billy Peyton." The door opened and her dark form waved to me from the porch. I dismounted and made my introductions. She demurely took my right hand after transferring a small pocket pistol into her left.

She closed the curtains and stoked the fire. I re-

layed my most recent adventures, leaving out my
Rocheport experience. She fixed me a bite to eat as
I secured my horse back in the draw. After eating,
we sat by the dying embers.

"You have had quite a time, Billy," she said. "This
war has made a man out of you. Not too long ago
you was just a runny nosed kid, always staring at me
with them cow eyes of yours." As she spoke she
poured two tumblers of dark whiskey.

"To your health," she toasted. Laughing, she continued, "I heard about your escapade over at the
Dutch barn dance. You really think you could hide
that? Why Billy, that's been the talk of the county!"

I gulped and felt flush, glad that the darkness hid
my embarrassment. "Yes, ma'am, that was not my
finest moment."

"Well, Billy," she said, "you have had more troubles in your life than most, and you are young. How
old are you, Billy?"

"I'm just about 19, Ma'am," I offered.

"Cut the ma'am, Billy, I ain't much older than
you."

She stood, and sipping the last of her drink she
said, "It's time for bed. Usually when I entertain my
Confederate guests they hide in my secret room I
have under my bed. Come see." We entered the bed-
room and she pointed to a pretty little Jenny Lind
bed. "Give me a hand, we move it to the left."

Under the bed was a rag rug. Under the rug was
nothing that I could see but floor, until she reached

down and pushed one of the floor boards. This exposed a latch which opened a trap door leading down into a small room containing a pallet of blankets, a lamp and a slop jar.

"As you can see, Billy, anyone hiding down there is my prisoner, but they're safe." I acknowledged that would be the case.

All evening I had felt a tension between us. I knew there was no reason for her to be angry with me, and yet this beautiful vivacious woman brought out insecurities unbefitting a partisan ranger.

"Come here, Mr. Peyton," she beckoned.

A hot flash shot through my body and there was a stirring in my loins. I had had a crush on this woman as a boy, and now she had called me to her as she pulled the ribbon from her hair. Her cascading curls created the most erotic sensation I had ever experienced. I had never been with a woman before. Yes, there had been plenty of opportunities since our guerrilla band held company with fallen doves, but I had never had the inclination or maybe the nerve. To wallow in the lap of some tawdry whore had no appeal to me. Some of the stories of my compatriots regarding their sexual adventures did stimulate, but I was also keenly aware of the health dangers of these activities. Far too many of our soldiers had fallen, not to the minie, but to the rampant social diseases of the day.

But Lord, this was a far cry from the brothel cribs. This was Miss Mandy Ross of Franklin who I

had lusted after in my youth and now the widow
Hawkins whose brief marriage had been interrupted
by a Yankee cannon ball. This was the beautiful
Mandy who had now slipped out of her dress and
stood in front of me silhouetted by the firelight.

The morning was dark and overcast. I awoke
alone in the bed as memories of the night's activities
flashed before me. My God! Her voice called from
the kitchen,

"Up and at 'em, soldier boy! Get in here. I've got
coffee."

I drank my coffee and watched her through different eyes. We didn't say much, I didn't know what
to say and she had no need. After breakfast she
said,

"Billy, you must skedaddle before that Yankee patrol comes nosing by here. They will before long."

"Yes ma'am, I mean Mandy."

As I rose and buckled on my Colts she said, "Mr.
Peyton I thank you for last evening. I ain't no saint,
but you must know I don't make a habit of making
love to my guests. What we done ain't a regular oc-
currence. I knowed you have admired me for years,
and I appreciate it more than you'll ever know. I
needed what you gave me and I'm pretty damn sure
you needed me. I'm real proud to have been your
first. I like you, Billy, and I pray you won't get killed.
If you don't, more than likely I'll be here iffen you
need me. Now get!"

With that speech ringing in my ears I stumbled

Billy's War

out into the morning mist.

Chapter Fifteen

I arrived back at our hideout in Jackson County just in time to join the boys and make the long trek down to the safe haven of Sherman, Texas. After so many days in the saddle it seemed as if I had grown to my horse, so I was looking forward to settling down for awhile.

My spirits were high as we slowly made our way south, but not without encountering some Federals. We were not really interested in fighting and it seems that went for the enemy as well, with a few exceptions.

Upon reaching Bates County we discovered that there were over four hundred Federals camped at Prairie City. Food for our men and horses was scarce since this was the area the Federals had looted and burned thanks to General Order Number 11. We were traveling in small groups so as not to raise suspicion and basically to keep out of harm's way. We were heading for some rest and relaxation and didn't want any bluecoats to interfere with our plans.

My companions on this particular day were my

old friends George Wigginton, Dave Hilton and
George Langdon. Dave's mother and sisters had
moved to the area to stay with her sister's family after their Jackson County farm had been burned to
the ground.

After crossing the Marais des Cygnes River of my
dark memories we decided to drop in on Dave's family. We spent a couple of days at their place, camping out in the woods during the day and sleeping in
the barn at night. The morning we were to leave
opened with Dave's sister yelling,

"The Yankees are coming!" Sure enough, I saw
about fifty men on foot no more than seventy or
eighty yards away. Our mounts were saddled and
ready. Mrs. Hilton had even presented us with a
ham that was secured in a pouch on Dave's horse. I
don't know how those Federals had got wind that we
were there, but they surely did. The leader yelled,
"Don't be afraid, we are your friends." George
Wigginton jumped on his horse yelling, "Friends be
damned!" and bolted from the barn shooting both of
his Navy colts. I followed almost on top of him but
my pistols failed to fire. The heavy dew and moisture
in the air must have dampened the powder. Bad
timing, as we needed to make as much noise as possible hoping to scare them away. I need not have
worried about noise because the line of Feds belched
hot lead the moment we hit the lane. Dave Hilton
was a bit smarter than we were because he walked
his horse out the back door and keeping the barn

between him and the shooting walked safely into the woods.

Having survived the first volley we were safely on our way and about a mile down the road we met up with Dave, who said, "Too close a call for me. I guess it'll be some time before I see my Ma again."

"Let's not be so sure," I said. "We need to see what they are going to do to your family." So we did what we do best. We unsaddled our horses and rested and waited until dark. George reminded us more than once that we were really on vacation and that life would be very good in Texas, and that we were damn fools not to be high-tailing it down there right now. But Dave and I wore him down, at least enough to get him energized regarding our evening plans.

There were no campfires near the house so we knew the majority of the militia had gone back to Prairie City. This didn't mean that the coast was clear, however. Leaving the horses at the tree line we carefully approached the house. My reloaded and hopefully now functional Navy Colts felt cold and re-assuring as we neared the barn. Inside, we discov-ered three fine Federal horses. George Wigginton whose love of horseflesh overshadowed any other passion, was for a quick assault. But after we con-sidered the possibility of quick and sudden retribu-tion we decided to wait it out. Back in the woods, we settled in for the night. At daylight we could see the house come alive with the normal activities of the day.

The Federals stood out in their blue coats as one by one they visited the outhouse and then the barn. Walking our horses through the wood to the other side of the house, we rode about two miles down the road leading to town where we waited while the god-damned Yankees ate our breakfast. It was about an hour and a half later before we heard the clip clop of horses and rustle of tack heading our way. The men were having a fine old time, bleating on about this and that, smoking and cock sure of themselves after intimidating old women and children. As the party came abreast we slowly rode out and stopped in front of them. The Federals stopped short in front of the potential firepower of six Navy Colts. My bush-whacking hunting shirt pocket also contained four extra loaded cylinders I could pop in if needed.

But then George Wigginton says, "Well, I'll be damned. It's John McDowell. How you doing, John?"

It seems that McDowell had gone with General Price back in '61, but following Lexington he had gone to Independence and got himself paroled. George relayed this information as we relieved the three of their weapons. I asked what they had done to those innocent womenfolk we had imposed on by sleeping in their barn. The lieutenant said they had no idea who the rebel bunch was that had stolen their food and forced them to care for them.

"Well, that's true," Dick said with a sideways look

and a wink, "but it looks like you helped yourself to
their smokehouse as well," pointing towards two
large gunny sacks.

The captives remained mute, so Dick spoke up.

"Well this is what we are going to do. You two,"
pointing to the lieutenant and the corporal, "take off
your boots and get the hell out of my sight." Pointing
to McDowell, he said, "Now John, you grab the reins
of those horses and we will ride on for awhile. I
know you ain't one of these blue coats, really. They
must of forced you to be part of this raid. So welcome back to your roots." And off we went.

We stopped back at the farm delivering the stolen
hams we had recovered. Dick kissed his family
good-by. Mrs. Hilton insisted I take one of the hams
which I tied to my saddle bag.

"I thought you all didn't know these folks," John
McDowell muttered.

Back on the road again the only thing holding us
up from our trip was that traitor John McDowell because we really didn't trust him and didn't know
what to do with him. Toward nightfall as we neared
the Barton County line we dismounted to rest and
relieve ourselves. McDowell said he had to go himself, so we allowed that he could do that, as it actually seemed to be a good thing for all of us to do. I
said I would do the honors of watching our friend
John and the both of us headed into the brush.
John was going about his business so I squatted
down to do the same. No sooner than I got started,

that sonofabitch pulled a pocket Colt out of his boot and shot me in the ass. I fell down right in the middle of my shit. I could not believe this was happening. I couldn't feel any pain so I thought that maybe he missed and the worse part was having to wallow in filth. But he did hit me, taking about an inch off my butt cheek. Then the road exploded with sound and fury.

I stood up with my pants still down and hobbled toward the racket. By the time I arrived there was silence. John McDowell was sprawled out in the dirt. He was not moving. In fact, he would never move again.

The two Georges and Dick were grinning.

"Hey, Billy, you forgot to wipe," Dick said. I didn't laugh as I hobbled into a creek and tried to clean myself up.

Shortly thereafter, we found a partisan household that put us up for a day or two while I recovered. The shot had gone clear through my right cheek, which now burned like hell and complicated matters on horseback. I just about passed out when they drenched the wound in whiskey, but all things considered, I was very lucky. As far as I know they never found the body of that ass-shooting bastard John McDowell. The partisan family gave me an extra wool blanket to sit on and before long we were able to continue our trip to Texas.

During our Texas Christmas of 1863, two memorable events occurred. First off, the good people of

Sherman invited us to the largest and grandest ball I
had ever seen. It was a fine event, attended by many
young ladies from the area. But I couldn't help but
wish that the widow Hawkins was there to brighten
my celebration of the birth of the Christ.

The other event of that Christmas season was the
marriage of our own Captain Bill Anderson. We all
attended that affair and a fine time was had by all.
Again, memories of that wild night with Miss Mandy
interrupted my concentration during the nuptials.

Beside Sherman, another Texas town was favored
by our Missouri contingent. A fellow by the name of
John Shirley had operated the Shirley House Tavern
back in Carthage. Apparently divining the dark days
that would befall that bastion of secession he picked
up stakes and moved to Scyene, Texas and resumed
his tavern business. His daughter Myra Maebelle
Shirley was a handsome and vivacious teenager who
was smitten with our Missouri boys. Miss Shirley fell
head-over-heels for our fellow bushwhacker Cole
Younger who was a frequent visitor to the newly established boarding house and tavern. We all stayed
there from time to time. I always suspected that she
and Cole had much more than a casual friendship,
even though she married another man from our
bunch by the name of Jim Reed. After the war it was
rumored that her daughter was Cole's and not Jim's,
but Cole denied it. Myra Maebelle Reed herself became better known in later days as the notorious
Belle Starr.

Colonel Quantrill's camp was south of the Red River and our band was quite comfortable there. News of the war in the east was not very heartening, but our war was more personal and immediate.

The Texas rest had allowed my wound to heal. After years of fighting I was becoming more and more aware of the dangers inherent in my current vocation. I had killed men and had seen friend and foe alike meet their maker in some incredibly bloody fashion, but I never thought any harm would come to me. Again, the naivety of youth, I guess. But my wound had sobered me.

As the winter lingered troubles between our factions began to surface. Power struggles emerged and often things got ugly. So many of the original members of our band, 'the old men' we called them, were gone.

The commander of the Confederate sub-district of north Texas was not all that impressed with us, joining the Federals by calling us Missouri bushwhackers, and I guess for good reason. There were all too many robberies by these drunken youths that had nothing to do with anything but thuggery.

And there was some agreement by Confederate citizens that the Lawrence raid had gone way too far beyond the accepted conduct of the war. The citizenry was also growing disillusioned following the 1863 defeats at Vicksburg, Chattanooga and Gettysburg. A significant number believed that continuing guerrilla activity was doing more harm than good, and I was starting to believe this to be the case as well.

Yes, I had more than my fair share of the bushwhacking trade, but I soothed my conscience by holding to the belief that my actions were justified. The Unionists had taken everything I loved away from me and I just couldn't fathom how I could let them get by with it. But honestly, I was also getting a little tired of sleeping in the woods, starving most of the time and occasionally being fired upon by superior forces.

General Sterling Price, the acting military commander of Trans-Mississippi Confederate forces, asked Quantrill to reduce the number of his partisans by transferring most of them to the regular army. The reorganization officially promoted Quantrill to colonel, George Todd, one of his long time associates to captain and Bill Anderson to first lieutenant.

Not long after this a disagreement developed between the newly promoted and newly married Bill Anderson and Colonel Quantrill. It seems our leader had mellowed somewhat during our stay in Sherman but this was not the case with the bloodthirsty and volatile Anderson nor the reckless and wild teenage bushwhackers who followed him and made up his forces. Anderson railed against Quantrill, accusing him of cowardice.

Numerous personality conflicts and differences in leadership styles had also developed between Ander-

son and Todd. George Todd had ridden with Quantrill for years and was one of his most trusted lieu-
tenants, his right-hand man. But this was soon to
change.

Our colonel had tried to assert a modicum of discipline over his command, but this was fast becoming a daunting task. Todd, desiring to assert his independence, sided with Quantrill and a lackluster
and almost comical shootout occurred between the
two factions. No one was injured but this cemented
the split and Anderson and his followers headed
back home to the Perche Hills. Lt. Anderson left his
bride, who was working at a saloon in Sherman
which was also owned by a former Missourian. It
seems that the marriage didn't do much to soften his
disposition, but most of us believed he loved her, at
least in his own way.

Finally, so many complaints regarding the conduct of Quantrill's boys had reached the general that
he had no choice but to take some action. We all accompanied our colonel over to Bonham which was
the general's headquarters, and waited to hear the
outcome of the meeting. Lo and behold the general
had Quantrill arrested. The story went that after he
was arrested the general invited Quantrill to supper.
Our colonel refused the invitation, so the general left
Quantrill under guard, but that didn't last very long.
Quantrill overpowered the guards and busted into
the street, hollering that the whole kit and caboodle
of us was about to be under arrest and that we

should get the hell out of there, which we did in a cloud of Texas dust. A detachment of militia was send after us, but nothing much happened.

I puzzled about what a shame it was that we were fighting each other instead of the Yankees, but that's human nature, I guess.

At any rate, before long we headed home back though Indian country where we didn't have to worry about the Confederate militia or Federals either.

The spring of 1864 was as fine as it gets in Missouri. Our old "stomping grounds" were a welcome sight. The new Union general in Kansas City had loosened the iron hand of General Ewing's Order Number 11, and was allowing folks to return to their homes. Of course there were not many homes to return to since the Kansas Red Legs had burned and pillaged their way through these counties.

Wintering in Texas had mellowed my senses and dulled my hate for the Yankees, but riding back through the devastation in Vernon, Bates, Cass and Jackson counties inflamed my anger all over again. The countryside was littered with stark silhouettes of the chimneys of burned out houses. No crops were planted. No livestock roamed the prairies. It was a desolate place. Besides, this Order number 11 had worked because there were no citizens to hide us and no food for our men and our horses. We also learned that Jackson County was now host to over a thousand Union cavalry from Colorado whose sole purpose was to wipe out bushwhackers. We were accustomed to evading large blue jacket contingents, so we simply broke up into our small squads and arrived back home in Lafayette County without incident.

In March, the Confederate governor of Missouri in exile, Thomas Reynolds, who had assumed the office on December 6 following the death of Jackson from cancer followed by pneumonia, had encouraged Quantrill to join the regular army. George Todd was basically running the everyday operation of the command anyway, so Quantrill was considering the move. Todd was also getting a little bit big for his britches. He started to believe that he should be in charge and that Quantrill's leadership no longer met his approval.

The "straw that broke the camel's back" came about over an altercation at a card game between Todd and Quantrill. Card playing probably led to many deaths, and some of us swore that cards were more dangerous than Yankees. Many a good boy had fallen dead on the table over a question of cheating.

I was watching from the back of the room as tempers escalated. Quantrill threw his cards on the table and allowed he wouldn't play any more unless Todd shaped up. More words were exchanged in which Quantrill said he wasn't afraid of anyone. Todd drew his pistol and asked if Quantrill was afraid of him.

We all knew a couple of things. First, our colonel was not a coward. Second, we knew that Quantrill might be a dead man in a matter of seconds. Quantrill knew Todd very well, and acknowledged he was afraid of him. Todd put his pistol away and Quantrill rode away.

I didn't know what to do. Colonel Quantrill had always been good to me. He was an intelligent man and a fair leader. Todd was illiterate, crude and sporadic. Later a bunch of us were talking about the situation in which we had found ourselves. It was becoming clearer and clearer that we were embroiled in a lost cause. Dave Hilton opined that the war was damn near finished and that he guessed all he could do was to kill as many Yankees as he could. He allowed that he would also relieve them of their wealth and raise holy cane in the process. I said that George Todd surely was the man for him, but that I just didn't have it in me anymore. I had reaped heavy revenge on my personal enemies and would go home if I could. Someday I would like to rebuild the family homestead if the Yankees would let me.

Chapter Sixteen

The next day I lit out on the trail of Colonel Quantrill. I found out that Quantrill, his teenage companion Kate King, and a handful of loyal partisans were headed to my old Howard County hideout in the Perche Hills. We would bide our time safe and reasonably comfortable this early summer. I was tempted to strike out and visit the widow Hawking in Franklin, but Union troops were keeping a close eye on just about anyone with a Confederate connection. The Yanks were also aware that rebels inhabited the Perche Hills area from time to time, but they also knew a death trap when they saw one. It was said that Mandy was still above suspicion. Never the less I longed to relive that night with that amazing woman. I also feared that she had taken up with someone more mature and established than this Howard County bushwhacker.

As we hid in the hills that summer Todd and his followers stayed active, causing as much havoc as possible. They ambushed patrols, wagon trains and stagecoaches. No telegraph wire was safe. All this activity energized the Colorado units and they struck

with a vengeance. The plan was to engage the
bushwhackers in bushwhacker fashion, using our
tactics. Major General William S. Rosecrans was the
newest of a line of Union commanders who discovered that bushwhackers were not easy to bush-
whack. Time and time again the Union suffered
losses to Todd's raiders. It soon became clear that
though the Union controlled the towns, Todd owned
the countryside.

Our spirits rose when we learned of General
Price's plan to march into Missouri and take the
state back from the union. The Pro-Confederate partisans celebrated as best they could. Richmond and
Atlanta still held firm and now there was a chance
that Missouri would be 'liberated.' I became increasingly bored and restless as time idly slipped by in
our Perche camp. I finally approached Colonel
Quantrill and announced that I would be leaving.
The evening before I left the band, reminding me a
great deal of the classic story of Robin Hood and his
merry men, hosted a little farewell party. I was
vague regarding my future plans, not wanting to hurt
the colonel's feelings. I reckoned I might join up with
General Price. My actual intention was to hook up
with Bill Anderson who I had heard was operating up
around the pro-southern village of Waverly.

I was not aware of the atrocities Anderson and
his guerillas were heaping upon the inhabitants,
both military and civilian, of Johnson and Lafayette
counties. Had I known I believe I would have stayed

in the relative comfort of Perche, where I could at least visit my kinfolks from time to time. But I didn't. My restless nature overcame my common sense and I headed out seeking another adventure. I headed north into Randolph County where I met up with Anderson's outfit on 15 July, 1864 at the town of Huntsville, Anderson's boyhood home.

I found Captain Anderson on the front porch of the general store. Fortunately he recognized me, but didn't remember that I had sided with Colonel Quantrill. His men were systematically taking the town apart. Stores were looted and the main street was cluttered with debris.

'What have I got myself into,' I wondered. This wasn't war, this was just a bunch of ruffians out of control. My first inclination was to get away as fast as I could. But if I did, suspicions would be raised and I probably would be shot as a traitor. Some of the 'old timers' knew me, but there were others that were new and taking their cue from 'Bloody' Bill Anderson. More blood was added when a Union supporter salesman was discovered and killed. So there was not much to do but find a couple of old friends and go get drunk at the hotel where the drummer's body had just been removed.

The next day our bushwhacking band saddled up. Anderson had relieved the community of $50,000 in Yankee greenbacks, my companions hauled away all they could carry and I left with only a world class hangover. But all was not well. A Federal detachment had picked up our trail and I found myself engaged in a running gun battle, again! It wasn't as exciting as it had been when I first started my guerrilla career. Now, I just didn't want to get shot. My companions were littering the road with cast off loot to lighten their loads and eventually the patrol gave up the chase.

We went down to my southern sympathizing town of Rocheport where I had another happy reunion with my mother, aunt and all the family. My fellow marauders occupied their time by resting and shooting at riverboats as they steamed up and down the Missouri River. My exploits at the Dutch barn dance the year before still embarrassed me as the citizens of Rocheport were fond of reminding me of my folly.

I stayed behind with my family for a few days while Bloody Bill looted the Village of Renick and cut the telegraph wires.

A Union detachment from Glasgow thwarted a raid on the town of Allen, eventually killing two of my new friends and wounding several more. Believing that the bushwhackers had tucked tail and run, the Feds packed up and headed back to Glasgow by the Fayette Road. As events turned out, this was a major underestimation of Bloody Bill's grit.

As I laid around with my family daydreaming about the widow Hawkins, Anderson's party surprised the Glasgow troops whose single shot rifles were again no match for the bushwhackers' best friends, the Colt revolvers. Two soldiers were killed there. One of Anderson's men that I couldn't stand was Archie Clement, called Little Archie, who took it upon himself to scalp the dead men. I had heard that this was a signature trademark of his, but I was never anywhere near when he committed these barbaric acts. He was a psychotic killer who, believe it or not, made Bloody Bill look like a Sunday school teacher.

Shelbina was next on Anderson's list. A 150 foot long railroad bridge over the Salt River was burned along with several out buildings. For the next couple of weeks the Anderson gang, for I now know that is what they were, terrorized the citizens of Huntsville and Macon county. Bill's brothers and his followers had now joined the force, increasing the raiders numbers and ferocity.

To the uninitiated the ground covered by our men must seem impossible, but we thought nothing of it. Finally, ashamed of my lounging with my loved ones in Rocheport, I donned a Yankee uniform, which is what we all wore these days, and finally caught up with my companions just in time to join the burning and killing as we swept through Ray, Clay and Platte counties. There was only a feeble resistance and I admit that I gained some pleasure from burning the barns of Union supporters.

In mid August we stopped. camping about ten miles north of Liberty. We rested on our butts as well as on our laurels. In spite of some of the atrocities perpetrated by a few of my fellow partisans I felt

a certain amount of pride in what our band had ac-
complished. We had traveled over three hundred
miles across northern Missouri. Every telegraph had
been cut, every railroad bridge and depot had been
burned. We had looted and sacked towns and
steamboats, destroying millions of dollars in property. We had successfully fought the Union militia
and some of our boys had slaughtered and robbed
Yankee-supporting civilians. All in all, it was one
hell of a summer!

The loyal citizens would agree, if for different reasons. George Wigginton, who honestly was more
pleased and excited about the raid than I was, came
running up with a copy of the <u>St. Joseph Herald</u>. It
was the August 10th issue and the editors summed
up fairly accurately the feelings of Missouri Unionists. Basically, the article stated what we all knew,
that William Anderson was a heartless cold-blooded
bushwhacker. The editor waxed eloquent about how
Quantrill and Todd languished in the shadow of our
black clad leader.

Most of the boys were quite prideful about being
hooked up with this guerrilla Anderson. For me it
was just a means to an end. I had got into this
bloody business for revenge and I guess that's why I
continued to stay.

The heat was on from the Union forces, but there
really wasn't much they could do about us. The local militias were scared shitless of us and the majority of the population supported us. The militia ranks

also contained a significant number of "Paw-Paws." These were Southern sympathizers who had been forced into service for the Union. The alternative generally was a noose. We also had better weapons and rides. Our campaign across the state gained a great deal of positive publicity for the cause and young men from all over were flocking to join up with us.

Of all the Federal units the Kansans were the most hated. They were far worse than our bush-whackers. For years they had run roughshod over Missourians, believing that everyone in this state was a rebel, which gave them impunity in their des-picable treatment of our citizens. It made no never mind, if you were woman or child or old. If you had something they wanted, it was gone.

We retaliated when we could. The good book, I think, says an eye for an eye. That was good enough for me. I didn't approve of the scalping and wanton killing of innocent Union folk like some of our boys did, but so be it. War is war, ain't no getting around it.

One day a couple of my old friends came riding into our camp. The James brothers had been hiding out on the family farm up near Kearney when they learned about our recent exploits. Jesse told me they had come to join in on the fun. Considering what he had been through it's no wonder he was looking forward to having some fun. In fact, he was not alone. We were all full of ourselves and proud of

our righteous cause. Our ranks swelled to over a
hundred which was more than half as much more
than usually rode with us. Our leader had taken
some time away from marauding but as they say, all
good things must come to an end. We left our comfortable camp and headed east on the warpath once
more.

One evening I was whittling and spitting with
Frank James' younger brother. We were swapping
stories.

"Well, Jesse," I said as I placed a log on the fire,
"What brought you here at such a tender age?"

"Like you, Billy, I was not a villainous border ruffian," he said with a wink. "I was just 14 and too
young to join up, but Frank, he lit off and got into
that ruckus down at Wilson's Creek. You was there,
so you know what that was like. Then some Union
militia came looking for him and scared the bejesus
out of my Ma and sisters. The Federals took my
stepfather, one of the kindliest physicians you done
ever saw, and set out to get him to tell them where
Frank was. Hell, he didn't know. None of us knew
his whereabouts. But they tied a rope around his
neck and hung him seven times. They almost
choked the life out of him. Then they up and left
him for dead. He didn't die, but he ain't been able to
do anything since then. He just sits and rocks in
that old chair on the porch. Poor Ma. Terrible thing.
I'm out in the back 40 plowing and don't know a
thing. Those bastards come riding up and they say

for me to tell them where Frank is. For God's sake, I
don't know either. Then they damn near whipped the
shit out of me but I still couldn't tell em where Frank
was because I didn't know. Eventually they quit
their fun and rode off, leaving me bloody and lying in
the dirt. I could hardly walk back to the home place.
It took me about a week to heal up and that's when I
figured it was time for Jesse James to bring about
some justice. When I was able I struck out for here
on foot with nothing but my Pa's double barrel shotgun.

"As luck would have it, a couple of them soldier
boys came riding along. I seen 'em first and hid in
the bushes not more than two feet from the road.
They was laughing and talking about the fine ole
time they was going to have in them sportin' houses
in Westport. Except they never got the chance to get
either pleasure or the clap because I jumped out of
the brush and blew both of them to hell. I was kind
of surprised. I didn't feel bad. The biggest thing I
ever killed was a shoat and here I've killed these two
Federal bastards and I feel really good. I mean I felt
great!"

I jumped in, saying, "I know exactly what you
mean. It was the same with me. I felt righteous.
And I still do."

Jesse nodded in agreement. "Yes, sir, I killed 'em
dead in their tracks. They never knew what happened. And I got two fine horses and their gear. I
stripped them and carried them into the hollow. I

buried their clothes. After that I traveled at night and lo and behold, here I am."

*   *   *

In Ray County we hit a Union camp and killed five men, which got General Fisk to telegraph the garrison in Chillicothe to come after us. From Ray County we continued on to Carroll County where a contingency from Chillicothe experienced a bitter lesson. We drove them off, killing more than a dozen. One of the young firebrands who had just joined us went charging into the blue bellies and paid with his life. He was a brave soul but really stupid. You wait until they shoot their first volley and then charge them like the devil himself. I think I'd become callous, because all this killing just didn't affect me like it used to.

Young Jesse got shot through the chest and I was knocked from my horse by some buckshot, but only a few of the pellets broke the skin. We were the only boys wounded, so Captain Anderson left us in the care of a partisan family in Carroll County to recuperate. This was the second time I had been shot, and even though it wasn't life threatening, it was very painful. Jesse had it a lot worse than I did, but we were young and healthy and figured we would heal quickly. What I hated most is that I was going to miss going though Howard County. I sure would like to visit the widow Mandy. I had kept my own counsel regarding that experience, but in our convalescence I confided in Jesse. He told me that he had no knowledge in these matters, but guessed it would be best if I didn't put too much into it. She was an older woman, a widow, and more than likely I wasn't the only man she had entertained in her Jenny Lind bed. I didn't much like to hear this kind of commentary, but there was a ring of truth to what my friend said.

Word filtered into our hideout that the militia was in full force and were scouring every nook and cranny for our forces. They knew where they had been because of the wake of death and destruction our boys left behind, but they just couldn't figure out where they were going. We learned that the Seventeenth Illinois had ventured into the Perche Hills and though experiencing casualties, had succeeded in scattering my erstwhile friends. This didn't mean much, however, as this is the way we always operated in Howard County. There were plenty of secessionists that would feed and protect us until we received the call to form arms.

My wounds became more serious than I had initially thought. Infection set in and I suffered from chills and fever. Our patient hosts, Eli and Martha Cooper, believed that we would be safe. We were holed up in their sturdy frame house in an isolated section south of Carrolton and this elderly couple seldom had visitors. The Coopers had no surviving children and the neighbors and local authorities suspected nothing. They had never owned slaves and did, in fact, support the Union. They were Douglas democrats, however, and had no truck with the radical republicans. They also let it be known to fellow partisans that the occupation of Missouri by military force was more than they could stomach. So they helped the cause whenever they could by supporting our irregular units.

Rumors of increasing violence circulated throughout the county. It seems that Bloody Bill continued to enhance his reputation with ever increasing exploits and alleged atrocities. I was starting to regret that I had not stayed with Colonel Quantrill. It seemed that Anderson's outfit had completely lost sight of our original objective and turned completely into a roving band of felons and murderers. I knew we were a bunch of hard cases, but I couldn't comprehend some of the stories Mr. Cooper would share. We heard how some of these boys plundered and killed just for the thrill of it.

Eventually our health improved to the point where we decided to leave the relative security of the Coopers and strike out for greener pastures. Those pastures turned out to be over at Jesse's home place near Kearney.

The neighborhood was buzzing with news, both good news and bad. The bad was that while Bloody Bill lounged in his self proclaimed capital of Rocheport, several of the fellows we were not acquainted with let their guard down and got themselves shot to kingdom come by the Federal mounted Ninth Missouri State Cavalry out of Fayette.

This hit our guerilla leader hard. Unfortunately for the Federals, any time they caused Bill Anderson pain his retaliation was threefold. The good news, at least for us, was that on September 23rd Anderson struck a Federal wagon train and shot up as many blue coats as he could find.

But the violence didn't end there. The troops from Fayette picked up the trail and eventually killed six of our boys. I guess these Yankees had learned a thing or two from some of our fellows because after killing them they scalped them.

Now the violence never seemed to stop. Both sides were having a heyday. I was getting tired of the whole mess. How did I ever get in this deep?

Back in Kearney more disturbing news reached our ears. It seems that the men killed were part of a new plan that Anderson had hatched up. Since he had declared himself the "King"of Rocheport he decided to levy a tax on the citizens. It was said to have been voluntary, but if anyone didn't contribute, well, Anderson's "tax collectors" would beat, kill and burn the homes of the reluctant citizens of his "kingdom."

This news sickened me, but I kept my thoughts to myself since Jesse and his family celebrated any pain, be it ever so small, upon Union supporters. Unfortunately, they seemed to ignore the fact that Anderson was doing this to our own southern supporters as well. I was glad to be out of the picture for

awhile. But again I was restless and I still believed
that General Price's upcoming invasion would liber-
ate the state. Price had asked Captain Todd and all
Missouri guerrillas to help prepare the way for him
by burning bridges, cutting telegraph lines and generally diverting Union troops away from his forces.
This sounded good to me. Quantrill had made an
uneasy peace with Anderson and to a degree everyone was cooperating. But not for long.

It looked like we were back in the Confederacy
until yet another power struggle erupted over strategy. Anderson and Todd wanted to attack Fayette.
Quantrill essentially said that the town was a for-
tress and there was no way a raid would succeed.
The captains again called Quantrill a coward, and for
the second time the colonel pulled up stakes and
rode away. This time I should have gone with him.
But I'm a fool.

The long and short of it was that Quantrill was
right. Unfortunately for me I wasn't aware of any disagreement among our leaders and arrived just in
time to kiss my kinfolk back in Rocheport and mount
up once more.

It was a reckless adventure. Captain Todd was
all about proving that he was a better man than that
"coward" Quantrill. Sure the town was fortified but
in our blue uniforms we held the element of surprise.
Of course that would be the case if everything went
as planned. And, of course, it didn't. One of our
trigger-happy teenagers jumped the gun and shot a

Negro in a Yankee uniform. This alerted the whole
garrison that was safe behind log walls. It was our
custom to ride into a town, shooting and hollering
and scaring the water out of the helpless militia.
That was back then, this was now and my Yankee
neighbors from Fayette shot the hell out of us. I
barely escaped the wall of hot lead that poured forth
from the do-or-die militia.

It didn't take long for those of us who survived
the ordeal to figure out that Todd and Anderson were
brave beyond all reason. Foolhardy was more like it.
We also understood that William Quantrill was the
smarter of the bunch. Back at camp we licked our
wounds and watched our leaders fester over this defeat. We had experienced the greatest defeat in our
bushwhacking career. Knowing when and where to
strike was our strength. Our captains had acted
foolishly and had failed to avenge the deaths of our
fallen comrades. In fact, the raid had added to the
toll of the dead and wounded.

Anderson was like a caged animal. The defeat at
Fayette only fueled his blood lust. And that is why I
turned up near the village of Paris with a large number of my fellow guerrillas out looking for trouble!
We got word that a newly formed Yankee unit, the
Thirty-ninth Missouri, was on our tail with orders
from General Fisk to exterminate us. We had been
looking for a fight and it looked as if we would get
one.

Our spies had told us that this bunch was so new

that they hadn't even received training. Most were mounted but they were really an infantry unit which meant they were armed with single shot Springfield rifles. These weapons were excellent for long distance fighting but worthless in cavalry engagements. I, for one, looked forward to meeting these untrained farm boys. It felt like I was back in a real military unit with a real military mission. No more plundering and looting for the spoils. This was a war with a noble cause and we would fight it honorably. Or so I told myself at the time. As it turned out, I was oh so wrong again.

I look back at that time in my life, and wonder how I could have been so stupid. I can rationalize about it as the excesses of youth, coupled with misplaced loyalties and the desire for revenge against those who had destroyed all that I loved. Here in the cold light of day I have to confront my demons and simply admit that I was just plain wrong!

It was the morning of September 27, 1864. I awoke with a sore back and a mild hangover. I had taken to dulling my senses with drink and I must have done a fairly good job of it.

On our way we had destroyed several miles of wire along the north Missouri railroad, but suffered the loss of twenty guerrillas. These Yankees were getting meaner and meaner. It was starting to seem as if this largest contingent of partisan rangers since Quantrill's raid on Lawrence might be chasing its own tail.

My excitement at the beginning of this adventure had quickly turned to disappointment and depression. The towns we passed were well fortified and besides the Thirty-ninth Missouri there were numerous units out scouring the countryside for us.

Todd asked Anderson if he would go over to Centralia and try to find out what progress General Price's invasion was making. He agreed to go, not so much to gain information as to gain revenge for his failure at Fayette. We left Young's Creek for a little over a three mile ride into the town. I felt a little sick, but I was used to it by now.

Centralia was a railroad town consisting of a new depot, two hotels, a couple of stores and a few houses. It didn't look to be very prosperous but it had avoided the ravages of war. It was just about ten o'clock in the morning when we rode into town unmolested. As was typical, and as we thought our right, we took what we wanted. Several railroad cars were discovered which contained crates of footwear and more importantly, for my fellow conquerors, a large barrel of whiskey. My alcohol-poisoned body cared not for this find but the rest jumped on it like a flock of buzzards on a dead coon. It wasn't long before those boys were in their cups. It's amazing how stupid folks act when they are drunk. And many of our unit were not all that stable when sober. Captain Anderson availed himself of a goodly helping of the brew. He, like most of us, was no stranger to drink, and made liberal use of this Yankee whiskey.

We heard the train coming up from the town of Mexico. Some of us who were relatively fit stacked ties on the track in front of the station. I had always been impressed by trains, even though I had never been on one. This one looked to be under full power and was headed full steam ahead. Apparently the brakeman and the engineer had not had time to co-ordinate their actions. Spotting our forces, the engineer had intended to smash the barricade and press on to the Union garrison at Sturgeon just a few miles away. The brakeman, however, applied his trade and the iron horse screeched to a stop. I must admit it was exciting. This powerful engine bearing down on us, belching smoke and looking like it would fly right by us. I jumped out of the way because I expected the ties to explode before us. But the train stopped. I wondered what the plan was or even if there was a plan. While the boys were busy relieving the passengers of their valuables, Bloody Bill, Frank James, myself and several others headed to the baggage car. The terrified agent opened the strong box which contained thousands of dollars. That crazy Archy Clements herded a party of unarmed soldiers off the train. Apparently these men were headed home to Iowa on leave. I thought reaping in that large amount of currency was a fair excuse for the raid but watching my companions steal watches and harass women and children disgusted me.

I was now ready for a taste of the hair of the dog. What I was witnessing wasn't war, it was sheer brutality. The cries of the innocent women and children reminded me of my own family's anguish so many years before.

The soldiers were ordered to remove their uniforms as Anderson watched from the far side of the train. He yelled at me to help separate the civilian men from the women and children. Those who refused to turnover their money were shot. The women's terror rose to a feverish pitch as they watched their unarmed love ones gunned down. Next the depot, warehouse and boxcars, even the one that had housed the demon whiskey were torched. The Union troops stood helpless in their underwear. Bloody Bill organized a firing squad but had 'Little' Archie Clement choose a Federal to exchange for one of our captured Rocheport 'tax collectors.' A sergeant by the name of Goodman was taken hostage and separated from the other prisoners. The scene turned uglier as it looked as if Bill was going to have the men killed. And sure enough, that is what he intended. Some of the men were stoic, accepting their fate, others begged to be spared and women and children wailed. Not normally squeamish, I backed away from this pitiful scene. I would be no part of this massacre. I was of enough sound mind not to be obvious in my pacifism, as I knew I could easily join the Federals if any of my companions sensed my disdain.

It was over in seconds. As the smoke cleared, the grisly sight of the dead and wounded sent a chill

down my spine. One huge Yankee fought his way
through the killers but was eventually brought down.
Someone counted twenty bullet holes in his now still
body. Some of my companions wandered through
the bodies mercifully finishing off the wounded. At
least I thought it was merciful, but they were just
having a gay old time.

Anderson then had the engineer fire up the loco-
motive, set the cars aflame and send the flaming
train towards the Sturgeon garrison. Anderson was
as happy as he had ever been. He had avenged the
death of his six tax collectors, burned the depot and
train and collected a substantial amount of cash.
Only the guerrilla exploits of Lawrence and Baxter
Springs, Kansas surpassed this raid.

We were ordered to form a column and headed
south. Back at Young's Creek most of the boys were
sleeping off the effects of their ill-gained liquor. I was
sober as a judge, even after a few swigs of old johnny
corn. I kept reviewing in my mind the previous
events that had shaken me to the depths of my soul,
that is, if I still had a soul.

The Yankees arrived in Centralia by mid afternoon. I reckon they were upset a plenty when they
spied the carnage that awaited them. The major in
charge decided to come after us which was not a
smart thing to do. He devalued the ferocity of our
guerrilla fighters, and the effectiveness of our Colt
revolvers. Down the Columbia road they came,
straight into our ambush. I swore to God Almighty

that if I survived this fracas, I would, as the spiritual says, 'study war no more.'

There was no more time to think. We readied ourselves and charged. Their officer had his men dismount and fix bayonets. I thought that was the stupidest thing I had ever seen, but also was glad that his tactics were left wanting. The long and short of it was that the day's slaughter wasn't quite finished yet. We slowly walked our horses in line of battle. The .577 Enfields they carried had a range of about three hundred yards so we weren't worried too much. From the south, George Todd's men advanced. From the north came the John Thrailkill party. The Feds were trapped.

John Thrailkill was a native Missourian who had moved around with his family, eventually marrying a gal from Saline County. At the beginning of the war he had joined the Missouri State Guard and was a veteran of Carthage, Wilson's Creek and Lexington, to name a few. At Springfield, he had been elected captain and saw further action in Arkansas. After the painful defeat at Pea Ridge he accompanied General Price's army out east where he was wounded at the battle of Corinth. He was sent back to Arkansas and served the Confederacy in the recruiting corps. In 1863 he was apprehended by the Missouri militia as he traveled in Clinton County in full Confederate uniform. He eventually ended up at the Gratiot Street Prison in St. Louis where he was sentenced to hard labor at a prison in Alton, Illinois. It didn't take him long simply to walk away from the quarry he was working in and escape, eventually ending up in Missouri back on recruiting duty.

To make a long story short, Captain Thrailkill eventually ended up in Platte County where he engaged in numerous military expeditions with our guerrilla leaders. Always more a military professional than a bushwhacker, he exercised a great deal of restraint over some of the more bloodthirsty raiders. Thrailkill and his men were not present at the Centralia slaughter, but their presence in the upcoming battle would cinch the victory.

Chapter Seventeen

Our force upped our pace toward the stricken Federals, raising a huge cloud of dust. The ferocity of our charge must have scared the hell out of those untrained recruits and they broke and ran. The few who stood their ground fired high, as was always expected. Off to my left I did see a couple of our boys fall. Some folks got lucky with their shots, I guess. And then the thrill of it all took hold of me and I started yelling with the rest. We hit the remaining enemy force at full speed before they could reload their rifles. I had been ordered to head for their horses whose holders had skedaddled at the first sound of gunfire. Over at the main fight, some of the braver Yankees fought, but the majority simply gave up. And then it was over.

We sat on our mounts and surveyed the wreckage. My battle crazed bushwhackers systematically finished off the confused survivors. Then we took off hell bent for leather back to Centralia to finish the job we swore the Yankees had started. Of course this was not the case since we had brought hell fire to Centralia first.

Most of us were still liquored up so my friends base instincts were in full bloom. The excess was extreme. Bodies had been scalped, mutilated and smashed. More than a hundred Union corpses littered the vicinity. We lost two dead and ten of us were wounded. Frank James was shot in the hip. I never thought I would welcome an injury but this time I did. One of the horse holders had shot me above my left wrist. It was a clean flesh wound that hurt like hell but didn't touch a bone. After my heart stopped racing, George Wigginton poured whiskey into the wound and I finished off the bottle, glad to have an excuse to miss out on the carnage.

In all, 146 soldiers and three civilians died in that day's action. Following this raid, Bloody Bill's reputation as the chief of the bushwhackers soared. An editorial in the <u>Leavenworth Daily Bulletin</u> held the opinion that Anderson had surpassed Quantrill in his quest for bloodshed.

We rode back to Young's Creek, where it had all begun. I was so drunk I could hardly stay in the saddle, but I was in good company since I was not the only bushwhacker with this problem. At least I had an excuse, I rationalized.

Following the massacre we headed back to Howard County. I was not feeling well and my wound throbbed like billy blue thunder since it had become infected, but I did alright and could keep up with the others, even at night.

It was either the second or third night on the road

– I was often delirious – when one of our scouts came riding up yelling that the Yankees were coming. Anderson led the way and everyone left the woods and headed back down the road. Well, that was everyone but me, because I was finished. No one seemed to care if I lived or died, not even George Wigginton. I was sick and tired and disgusted with the whole thing, so I simply slipped back into the woods. After a mile or so I unsaddled my trusty horse Blackey, that had carried me so many miles, spread my blanket and slept the sleep of the dead.

The next day I kept to the woods and evaded the Federals as I made my way back to a friendlier place. I hesitated to return to Rocheport and the bosom of my family because I figured the "king" would return and my bushwhacking career would start all over again. But I simply had had enough. Justice had been served as far as I was concerned. The war was over for me. Of course, this was easier said than done, since as a member of Anderson's bunch and a professed partisan, I was a wanted man. The only fate for me if caught was to shake hands with the grim reaper.

It turned out that my desertion saved my life since the Federals were hunting us down like hounds after the fox. The surviving guerrillas eventually arrived back in the Perche Hills where the blue coats feared to tread. I was taken in by a secessionist family in Higbee who my folks had known for years. When finally out of the saddle, my wound started to heal and I slept my cares away. Well, at least the memories of the horrors of Centralia faded a bit, even though it dominated the conversation throughout the area.

The band had experienced far too many close calls and narrow escapes, and it was time to split up and leave the area. After a few days of wandering, Anderson arrived at Rocheport in time to observe the destruction of his "kingdom." General Fisk had ordered the town to be burned to the ground. General Price, now located back in Boonville, issued an order for Captain Anderson and his men to hit the North Missouri Railroad again, especially the bridge in St. Charles County not far from the city of St. Louis. Price's orders elevated Anderson's stature even more. The one time convicted Kansas horse thief was now, for all practical purposes, a captain in the Confederate army.

The problem for General Price was, however, that Anderson was more intent on stealing than in bridge burning. After looting several villages Anderson joined Price's army at Waverly. He then roamed and plundered at will in the previously Union controlled area ranging from Boonville all the way to Independence. Back in Glasgow, he tortured a prominent Unionist, extracted several thousand dollars from his terrified relatives and raped a 13-year-old freed Negro house servant.

I had recovered enough to leave my newest safe haven and head for Tennessee where it was rumored that Colonel Quantrill was operating. Against my better judgment I figured I'd stop by the home place. It was common knowledge that the local enrolled militia kept an eye on abandoned rebel property, but I longed to go home since it had been a long time since my last visit.

I traveled at night and kept to the back roads and eventually turned up at my father's old friend's home. Surveying the place, which didn't look much different from the last time I saw it, and determining an absence of 'blue bellies,' I rode up and knocked on the door. An old black man who had been with the Squire as long as I could remember answered.

"Howdy, Ebenezer," I said.

"Why Massa Billy, you is a sight for sore eyes," he replied. As he ushered me into the parlor Squire Yates was wrapped in a blanket by the fire. Though Ebenezer had no problem recognizing me, if I hadn't been in his home I would have had no idea who this frail old man was. I had heard of people being a "shadow of their former selves" but this time I saw for myself the accuracy of this cliché.

We caught up on the news and sipped some of the finest brandy I had ever tasted. Since the squire was very rich and had accomplished a great deal of charitable good for most in need in the county before the war, he had continued to escape the Federals wrath. He had been a staunch Unionist even through he owned many slaves. By 1864 the occupational government had finally gotten around to freeing the slaves in Missouri officially. Most had no place to go and stayed where they were, doing what they always did. My aunt's Negroes had asked the squire if they could help out on his plantation and he consented. All had moved into his employ except the traitor, Jebodiah, who, I believed, had been directly responsible for the destruction of my family.

Often I daydreamed that if I ever found him I would shoot him at first sight. The squire said he had gone east somewhere and that none of the family had heard from him. I had loved his brothers as my own and his mammy was as dear to me as anyone in my life, but I swear I would not hesitate to do great bodily harm to him when and if I could.

The squire invited me to stay, saying I would be safe for the night, and I took him up on his offer. The help had already fed and stabled Blackey, so what else could I do. Who am I kidding, what a pleasure it was to experience the crispness of clean sheets again.

Over the course of our conversation with the squire and his family I learned that Miss Millicent had moved to St. Louis to live with her late husband's relatives. In the morning over a hearty breakfast, the squire filled me in on the fate of many of our neighbors. Among the list of injuries I heard about the well being of my old friends. I asked about the widow Mandy Hawkins. I mentioned that I had heard she was sympathetic to the Confederate cause. Mrs. Yates told me that she had learned that Mrs.

Hawkins had moved out east somewhere, following her new husband who was a major in the Confederate army. Upon hearing this an unexpected emptiness flooded over me. That woman still haunted me in the strangest ways.

After saying my goodbyes to the Yates's and our extended Peyton family, I headed out for the home place. As I cautiously rode down the lane past the generations of my ancestors buried in our cemetery bile rose in my throat and an anger I had not felt for some time rose within me. Apparently my emotions were no different from the time of my last visit. All was gone. The fields lay fallow behind the blackened hulks of what had once been a prosperous farm. I swore I would rebuild the place, though I had no idea how.

The biggest news any of us had heard since the Centralia massacre came about a couple of weeks after I had had a belly full of Bloody Bill and headed off to somewhat friendlier parts. On October 26, 1864, the Thirty-Third enrolled Missouri Militia caught up with Anderson in Gentry County not far from St. Joseph, Missouri. The Union leader had in fact learned his bushwhacking tricks and turned them with full force on the most notorious bushwhacker left in the state. A small contingent of pickets were sent out to lure Anderson and the boys back toward the town of Albany. Bill took the bait and rode straight into the muzzles of 150 Yankee rifles. Two bullets to the head ended his ruthless career.

His body was hauled to the courthouse at Richmond, Missouri where his personal belongings were displayed and his body photographed. Later his head was cut off and placed at the top of a telegraph pole as a warning to other guerillas, I suppose. After his burial folks said it was common for the good Union citizens and militia men to piss on his grave. I really can't say that I blame them. He was a no-good bastard, but at least he never killed me.

Earlier, Price's army had invaded Missouri once more. The second week of October they had moved past Boonville, sweeping past Glasgow and Lexington on the north side of the river and Sedalia to the south. A major engagement commenced at the Little Blue River in Jackson County. This river had been the scene of many partisan raids over the years.

A little more than two miles from Independence is where George Todd earned his just rewards. A sniper's bullet shattered his neck and he died a few hours later. Good riddance, I thought.

General Price's forces moved on from Independence down the Old Santa Fe Trail, eventually engaging the Federals at the Battle of Westport. The Confederates made a stand on the south side of Brush Creek but the overpowering strength of the Union forces prevailed and Price's army was forced to head south down the old Fort Scott Military Road. For all practical purposed, major Confederate operations were over in Missouri. Price and Marmaduke had failed to recapture their beloved state.

The winter of 1864-65 was difficult for me on so many levels. I had left Howard County and stealthily passed through Missouri and down past Crawley's Ridge in Arkansas to a friendly ferry that transported Blackey and me across the Big River into Tennessee, just above the occupied city of Memphis. There were plenty of secesh along the way who put me up, but it was a lonely and solitary trip. Heading east, I joined a company of Confederate Rangers who had been raising cane behind the Union lines. The Federals were spread thin as a majority of their regular troops had been sent east to participate in the siege of Petersburg, Virginia.

I eventually met up with some Missouri families who lived in Union City, Tennessee because the infamous Order number 11 had driven them from their homes.

Through the grapevine I eventually learned that Colonel Quantrill and his force were currently staying up around the village of Canton, Kentucky, not far from Hopkinsville. Several of the boys I had met decided they would accompany me so we set off up north. I had spent so much time in the saddle by now it was as if Blackey and I were one and the same.

I really liked my new friends, Henry Noland, Jim Little, John Baker and Foss Key. They were not cut from the same cloth as so many of our current Missouri bushwhackers were. I guess I am trying to say they were sane, Confederate patriots not fueled by blood lust. These boys were people to whom I could relate.

The trip into Kentucky provided us with a few adventures, some enjoyable and one very sad. Not far from Clarksville, Tennessee, we spotted a large contingent of Union cavalry. We were all wearing Yankee uniforms and were welcomed into their midst. There was a hotel and livery stable there where we stabled our horses. Our story was a simple one. We had been on furlough and were on our way back to meet up with our unit in Bowling Green.

This was a unit from Colorado and everyone was in high spirits with the current news that on April 9th, General Lee had surrendered to General Grant near the Appomattox courthouse in Virginia. I had known that even though our forces were resurgent out here, it was a different story in the east. The news was still a bitter pill to swallow. It looked as if my private war was also just about over.

We put on a good face for our Yankee hosts, but believe me it was not easy. For years these people had been my sworn enemies. The next day we continued our journey.

We had been following some Federal soldiers who stopped at a house along the main road. As we rode up there was some commotion and several of the Yanks ran out the back door. I didn't understand what was going on, especially since the Colorado boys had been so friendly and then out of the blue they started firing at us.

"What the hell?" I yelled. I could kick myself for dropping my guard. How stupid of me to trust these goddamned blue coats! "Sonofabitch!" As we were running for cover Jim yelled that he had been hit. We fired back and started to burn them out when they surrendered.

"Why the hell did you shoot at us?" I yelled. The gist of it was that they were spooked because they had heard that there were guerrillas wearing Yankee uniforms in the area and they figured we were after them. I guess I couldn't fault their logic.

"Hell!" I said. "Don't you know that the war is over?" Fortunately Jim's wound wasn't all that bad, so we paroled our captives and left them to care for him. We finally caught up with Colonel Quantrill all the way up north in Nelson County which was about fifty miles south of Louisville.

The Federals were as thick as thieves up there and I couldn't help but wonder why Quantrill wanted to be there, especially with the Confederacy crumbling like it was. But the war wasn't over for William Quantrill. The funny thing, though, was that now all the fighting was defensive. All our bushwhacking careers we had been on the offense, with occasional tactical retreats, but now we were on the run. Fortunately there were lots of Confederate sympathizers that gave us food, shelter and information regarding our pursuers.

Our Kentucky hosts welcomed us with open arms and in spite of being hunted like rabbits, all in all it was a beautiful spring. There was a great deal of talk about what to do. Some wanted to continue to fight, but most of us figured it would be best if we turned ourselves in. The problem for us was, however, that the damn Yankees had branded partisan rangers as outlaws. To be honest, there was a great deal of truth to this, but Quantrill's forces were a strictly-run military unit. That's what appealed to me about this command. One day a fellow came to our camp with news that Abraham Lincoln had been assassinated. This raised our spirits for a time. But after the excitement died down, I got to thinking and came to the conclusion that this might not have been such a good thing after all. It certainly would embolden the lively abolitionist republicans to seek revenge. Of course, they were determined to hang us out to dry anyway, so I guess it didn't matter much. Since we didn't seem to know what to do, we just continued to do what we were doing.

While we were flopping and twitching trying to figure out our options, Colonel Quantrill asked me, John Barker and several other young bucks to accompany him on a mission. George Wigginton had joined our group of ex-patriot Missourians and I for one was anxious for any action that would break the boredom of life in the camp.

It seems that one of our men from Missouri had been accused of robbing an old man of his only valuables. If I were riding with Todd or Bloody Bill they would have congratulated the alleged felon and asked for a cut. Not so Quantrill. He had never permitted robbery from innocent citizens and he said he was not going to start now.

We headed off up the Bloomfield Pike, but a sudden and heavy rain prompted us to seek refuge in Dr. Wakefield's barn. The good doctor had been a loyal Kentucky patriot and opponent to the republicans and their overlords.

There was a corn crib there and somebody started throwing corn cobs and before long all but Colonel Quantrill were involved in the boyish fun. We were so distracted that we failed to notice a company of blue jackets headed right toward us. We mounted up preparing to charge out the door with pistols blazing, like we always did. Unfortunately, the colonel's stirrup broke and threw him across his saddle. His horse bolted after the rest of us and before Quantrill could right himself a federal bullet hit him in the back. As we raced across the stubble field on the way to the woods and safety, our leader fell to the ground. He was moved to Dr. Wakefield's house where he was treated.

We raced back to camp to spread the news about our fallen comrade. After dark, I led Frank James, John Ross and some others back to the doctor's house. We wanted to move him to safety out of the clutches of the Federals, but Quantrill would have no part of it. He allowed that the war was over and that he was dying and that we needed to leave him alone. His last word was "Goodbye." And that was that.

But Quantrill wasn't going to die just yet. Several days later the Federals brought an ambulance and hauled him off to a military hospital in Louisville. A Catholic priest persuaded the authorities to move him to a Catholic hospital where he died on June 7, 1865. He is buried in the Catholic cemetery in Louisville. I had never heard anything about him being a papist, and I don't know if he was. But they had cared for him until the end and for that I was appreciative.

It was truly over now. George Wigginton, my old friend of so many campaigns, and I, along with some others we had picked up sought refuge back at Taylorville in Spencer County. A Confederate officer, Captain Stone, was there at the home of a prominent member of the community, a Mister Thurman. The Captain announced that he was going to surrender and advised us to do likewise.

Mister Thurman pointed out that this was not such a good idea since the Federals did not recognize Colonel Quantrill's command as a regular Confederate unit. This meant that we would be treated as outlaws and placed at the mercy of an overzealous martial law. Captain Stone said he would say that we were fresh recruits and that would make us legitimate Confederate prisoners, but I did not wish to take this chance.

Not long ago we heard how Jesse James had ridden into Lexington, Missouri, under a white flag and had been shot in the process. That's just what Jesse needed, one more wound, so he turned and got the hell away from the 'benevolent' victors. That boy had taken a lot of lead in this war and it's a damn good thing he healed well.

At any rate we decided not to chance a surrender in Kentucky, so we started on the long trek back towards home. We parted company with Captain Stone near the Town of Newcastle which is northeast of Louisville by about thirty miles.

Traveling was still dangerous as I retraced my path back into Arkansas. When I reached the Big River, I fell in with some boys on the run like me. Several had served in the fledgling Confederate Navy and a couple of these farm boys turned sailors had been with the famous Isaac Brown. I had no idea who this 'famous' man was but it didn't take long for me to get the story. He had lost his steam ram, the CSS Arkansas, which he had built and used effectively against the Federals on the river near Vicksburg. Brown was without a ship but he was not out of resources. Instead of warships he fashioned torpedoes out of whiskey demijohns and black powder. A five-boat Federal reconnaissance mission steamed up the muddy water of the Yazoo, and near the Confederate fortifications of Haines Bluff the ironclad USS Cairo hit one of the whiskey bottles and sank in less than ten minutes; hence Brown's fame.

I mentioned that I had a cousin who last I heard had been in the Confederate Navy up on the Yazoo. I said I hadn't heard from him in years and asked if

anyone had ever run into Jacob Walker. An older
man who had been listening to our conversation
stated that he knew the Walker boy and that he regretted that he would be the bearer of bad news. He
said he heard Jacob had been killed manning a battery at Haines Bluff. He didn't know any specifics
but he believed this to be true. I was heartsick with
this news but not altogether surprised. For years
now it had become patently evident to me that war
was fighting and fighting could lead to death.

Several years later I learned that indeed Jacob
had been killed in action but not the way relayed by
the old waterman on the banks of the Big River.

I discovered his fate by scouring through the official records of the United States Naval attack on New
Orleans that occurred sometime after Easter in
1862. Apparently there is a bend on the Mississippi
and our forces had built a couple of forts on the
scarce dry ground on either side of the river. Fort
Jackson and Fort St. Philip stood tall in the swampy
marshes and 'gator-infested bayous. Below these
forts our men had built a barrier of sunken ships
and a chain boom spanning the Mississippi. But
several factors worked against them.

The first was time. Two giant ironclads were being built but unfortunately they were not completed
in time to engage the Federal armada. Secondly, the
firepower of the Federal fleet could not be matched.
And thirdly, our hastily assembled Confederate flo-
tilla was also fighting a flood-gorged river. It all

spelled disaster for our navy. A dozen jerry-rigged sloops, cutters and gun boats faced Admiral Farragut's finest. I can only imagine the fate of the other vessels but the records show that the Confederate armored ram Manassas was battered into submission and ended her life stuck on a mud bank. Jacob's misfortune was that he ended up as an able bodied seaman on the side-wheel steamboat Governor Moore. The state of Louisiana had provided this vessel to assist in the protection of New Orleans and this is what they were about. In the darkness the Moore's two guns surprised and fired on the USS Varuna but missed. The Federals fired back and killed and wounded many a good man. The Moore's captain steamed ahead and fired directly into the Varuna with his forward gun. Heavy casualties were inflicted as the Moore then rammed the Federal amidships, but paid heavily from a Varuna broadside. Another Confederate gunboat rammed her for a third time and down she went into the Mississippi shallows.

This success energized the Moore's captain who wanted to continue the battle, but the first lieutenant at the helm opined that he would not stand by and be murdered and he tucked tail for the bank.

Shortly after that, five Yankee ships let her have it with all they could muster. In all, 57 of her 93-man crew were killed, 17 were wounded. The rest were captured or forced to slosh to safety through the swamps. Jacob Walker was listed among the dead.

His body was never recovered.

Back on the banks of the Mississippi, the same old muddy river that had contributed to my best friend's death, though I didn't know it at the time, I grieved for my lost friend and companion. But life goes on, and I needed to figure out what to do with mine.

I eventually found myself at Batesville, Arkansas, the town where Guffey died. George Wigginton and some other boys we had picked up along the way said it would be a cold day in hell before they surrendered and chose to head out after Captain Thrailkill and General Joseph Shelby on their expedition to Mexico. I still had a little Yankee gold in my pocket and a whole lot more of purloined treasure buried back in the Perche Hills so I figured I would stay here for a time in what I figured would be safe secessionist country.

At Batesville the Federal soldiers had treated the populace fairly in an unaccustomed effort to ease their suffering. And the suffering was great. Generals Lee and Johnston had surrendered and President Davis had been captured. On the other side, Lincoln had been assassinated and carpetbaggers eager for retribution and rewards were descending on us all.

I never thought I'd say this, but thanks to General Grant, attempts to prosecute Confederate leaders were squelched. Even though still in the army, he threatened to resign if amnesty was not given to the vanquished Confederates. Lincoln's successor,

President Andrew Johnson continued Lincoln's policy of forgiveness and reconciliation, but Congress refused to seat newly elected Southern legislators.

All the goings-on up in Washington City were fine and good, but for those of us everyday types all we wanted was to get done with the war, get the economy going and perhaps later pursue politics. But jobs were hard to get and even though the Federal government pursued a policy of benevolence the radical Republicans would have no part of it.

In late August I purchased a fine horse, not as trustworthy and battle tested as my old friend Blackey, but quality horseflesh never the less. It was time to reward my faithful companion with retirement, and I planned on entrusting him to my mother. I had decided to take my chances and return back to Howard County since I was running out of money and missing my family. I followed the doomed invasion route of General Price and eventually made it back home. I was hoping that my days as a bushwhacker would have been forgotten. I had not lived in one place for so many years and so much water had gone under the bridge I figured that no one would remember me as a companion of Bloody Bill. Fortunately all my old enemies were either dead or gone. No one seemed to remember the foul deeds I had been party to.

My story was simply that I had fought for the cause out east and the war was over and I was coming home. At Fayette I marched boldly to the court house, once a Yankee fort we had tried to destroy, and talked to the magistrate. I told him my fabricated tale. He listened politely, but seemed bored, which was all the better for me. No one knew or remembered me so he simply gave me the Oath of Allegiance to the United States and out the door I went, a free man. Freer than I had been in years, the weight was gone. The hate I had carried evaporated like the morning dew. God damn it, it felt good. I had heard the preachers talk about being born again. Well, sonofabitch, I was!

As I rode down the lane heading to the home place, I couldn't help but notice a bevy of folks working near a newly constructed barn. To my surprise a small cabin had been erected where the main house had stood. My mother and aunt, my little brother and all the sisters and cousins had returned to the place following the burning of Rocheport. With the financial help of Squire Yates and the return of the Negro Peytons the place had been rebuilt, crops were in and livestock grazed in the surrounding fields.

It was a sight for sore eyes!

As I tried to settle down to a normal life as the head of the household, I was still careful to maintain a low profile. The Unionists were in control and they harbored just about as much hate and distrust for us as we did for them. It was going to take a while for any semblance of peacetime normalcy to return.

Reconstruction provided us with a bitter pill. I had read in a classic many years earlier, before our library went up in flames, that 'to the victor go the spoils.' I was to learn that history certainly does repeat itself. The shooting was over, but the political war raged on. Lincoln's plan for a healing and conciliatory reconstruction died with him at Ford's Theatre. Some of our vanquished rebels were "ridden hard and put away wet."

But we survived, and with the help of the ill-gotten gains I unearthed from their hiding place in the hills, we even prospered. After the harvest of 1866 I lived my dream and attended the University to read for a law profession. I then moved back home and continued farming as well as hanging my shingle up in Fayette. I often strolled past the alley where the low-life Dutchman came to a deserved end, with nary a twinge of conscience.

I eventually courted a fine young lady from Higbee. We married and she kept the Peyton name alive with five sons and two beautiful daughters who married well. So many of my old friends and enemies alike were gone. My family never heard from George William. It was rumored that he had stayed in the Union army and had eventually settled in the northeast somewhere. I hate to say it, but the sonofabitch hurt my mother so much, that I just don't know what I'd do to him if he ever turned up. We mourned Guffey and Jacob and placed headstones in their memory down next to Pa at our family cemetery.

I'd run into George Wigginton every once in a while and catch up on the goings on. Frank and

Jesse continued fighting the war against the northern bankers and railoads, but that wss their business, not mine. Then Jesse was assassinated by the
coward Bob Ford and Frank James was acquitted of
charges of murder during a train robbery. It beats
all how things turn out. General Shelby testified as
a character witness at Frank's trial. Folks say he
was drunk at the time, but what the hell, Frank
walked away anyway.

Shelby's loyalty to Frank went way back. When
the James brothers were in Arkansas they encountered the General and his entire staff surrounded by
a large Union force. In spite of being outnumbered,
they charged the Yankees who scattered to the wind
as Shelby and company escaped.

Captain John Thrailkill remained in Mexico where
he became associated with the government and became a successful businessman. George had joined
up with General Shelby in Mexico when Shelby offered support to the Frenchman Maximilian but his
help was refused. However George and the other ex-
patriot rebels were given $50 each in gold for their
trouble. After the Mexicans won their independence
George returned to the states to farm. General
Shelby eventually became a United States Marshal in
Kansas City. He died of pneumonia at the age of 66.

As previously mentioned, General John Sappington Marmaduke, the young commander at the
'Booneville Races,' eventually became governor of our
fair state.

General M. Jeff Thompson, former mayor of St. Joseph and Missouri's swamp fox, was never able to recover economic security following the war. After a series of retail failures he was appointed as chief engineer on the Board of Public Works for the state of Louisiana. He retained this position until his death. He was 50 years old.

After briefly residing in Mexico, General Sterling Price 'Old Pap,' returned to the states. Thousands of Missourians donated money for the purchase of his house. He died at the ripe old age of 58.

Quantrill, Todd, Anderson and the other guerrilla leaders are all food for the worms. Following the 1876 failed bank robbery in Northfield, Minnesota, where the boys were severely wounded, the Younger brothers were sent to prison. Bob died there of tuberculosis. Jim committed suicide after his release and my friend and associate Cole ended up traveling the country telling of his adventures to crowds at Wild West shows.

I am an old man now. Over the years I have tried to forget some of the horrors of my past, but the memories will come rushing back to my consciousness at the most unlikely times. A smell, the sound of a gunshot, or a thousand other triggers will flood my mind with past events as clear as if they had happened yesterday. I still find solace in the hymn ' Ain't going to study war no more.'

But not long ago I was asked, if I had the opportunity, would I do it all over again? Would I? Damn right I would!

– END –

www.ingramcontent.com/pod-product-compliance
Lightning Source LLC
Chambersburg PA
CBHW020848090426
42736CB00008B/293